PLAYS

A SLEEP OF PRISONERS

THE DARK IS LIGHT ENOUGH

CURTMANTLE

CHRISTOPHER FRY

PLAYS

A Sleep of Prisoners

The Dark Is Light Enough

Curtmantle

OXFORD UNIVERSITY PRESS

LONDON OXFORD NEW YORK

1971

Oxford University Press

LONDON OXFORD NEW YORK
GLASGOW TORONTO MELBOURNE WELLINGTON
CAPE TOWN SALISBURY IBADAN NAIROBI DAR ES SALAAM LUSAKA ADDIS ABABA
BOMBAY CALCUTTA MADRAS KARACHI LAHORE DACCA
KUALA LUMPUR SINGAPORE HONG KONG TOKYO

ISBN 0 19 281110 X

A Sleep of Prisoners first published by Oxford University Press, London, 1951

The Dark Is Light Enough first published by Oxford University Press, London, 1954

Curtmantle first published by Oxford University Press, London, 1961; second edition 1965

The three plays first published as an Oxford University Press paperback 1971

PRINTED IN GREAT BRITAIN

CONTENTS

A SLEEP OF PRISONERS

A Play

To

ROBERT GITTINGS

Dear Robert

It is nineteen years this summer since you persuaded me to take a holiday from my full-time failure to make a living, and sat me down, with a typewriter and a barrel of beer, in the empty rectory at Thorn St. Margaret. I had written almost nothing for five or six years, and I was to write almost nothing again for five years following, but the two months we spent at Thorn, two months (it seems to me now) of continuous blazing sunshine, increased in me the hope that one day the words would come. It was all very well that I should look obstinately forward to plays which I showed no sign of writing. It was an extraordinary faith which made you also look obstinately forward to them. The ten years in which you loyally thought of me as a writer when clearly I wasn't, your lectures to me on my self-defensive mockery of artists, and those two leisure months under the Quantocks, were things of friendship which kept me in a proper mind.

We were talking even then, as we are talking, with greater instancy, now, of the likelihood of war. And I think we realized then, as we certainly now believe, that progress is the growth of vision: the increased perception of what makes for life and what makes for death. I have tried, as you know, not altogether successfully, to find a way for comedy to say something of this, since comedy is an essential part of men's understanding. In A Sleep of Prisoners *I have tried to make a more simple statement, though in a complicated design where each of four men is seen through the sleeping thoughts of the others, and each, in his own dream, speaks as at heart he is, not as he believes himself to be. In the later part of Corporal Adams' dream the dream changes to a state of thought entered into by all the sleeping men, as though, sharing their prison life, they shared, for a few moments of the night, their sleeping life also.*

C.

A SLEEP OF PRISONERS

First performed in Oxford at the University Church on 23 April 1951 and in London at St. Thomas's Church, Regent Street, on 15 May 1951 with the following cast:

Private David King	LEONARD WHITE
Private Peter Able	DENHOLM ELLIOTT
Private Tim Meadows	HUGH PRYSE
Corporal Joe Adams	STANLEY BAKER

The play was produced by Michael MacOwan

CHARACTERS

PRIVATE DAVID KING

PRIVATE PETER ABLE

PRIVATE TIM MEADOWS

CORPORAL JOE ADAMS

The interior of a church, turned into a prison camp. One prisoner, PETER ABLE, *is in the organ loft, playing 'Now the day is over' with one finger. Another,* DAVID KING, *is looking at the memorial tablets on the wall. Four double bunks stand between the choir-stalls. A pile of straw and a pile of empty paillasses are on the chancel steps.*

DAVID [*shouting up to the organ loft*]. Hey, Pete, come down and tell me what this Latin
Says. If it's Latin.

PETER [*still playing*]. Why, what for?

DAVID. For the sake of that organ. And because I want to know
If 'Hic jacet' means what it looks like.

[PETER *changes the tune to 'Three Blind Mice'*.

[*In a flash of temper.*]
And because I said so, that's what for, because
I said so! And because you're driving me potty.

PETER. Excuse me a minute: this is the difficult bit.

DAVID. If you want it difficult, go on playing. I swear
I'll come up there and put my foot through you.

[*As the playing goes on* DAVID *suddenly howls like a dog and starts tearing up a hymn-book.*

PETER [*the playing over*]. It's the universal language, Dave. It's music.

DAVID. Music my universal aunt. It's torture.

[*He finds himself with a page or two of the hymn-book in his hand.*

Here, I know this one.
[*Sings.*] 'All things bright and beautiful——'

PETER [*coming down from the loft*]. That doesn't mean you, Davy. Put it down.

DAVID. 'All creatures great and small—'
Well, one of those is me: I couldn't miss it.
'All things wise and wonderful——'

[CORPORAL JOE ADAMS *comes to the steps with more straw.*

ADAMS. Come and get it!

PETER What is it? Soup?

ADAMS. Straw.

PETER. Never could digest it.

[TIM MEADOWS, *a middle-aged man—indeed he looks well on towards sixty—limps up to the pile of straw.*

ADAMS. How's the leg feel, Meadows?

MEADOWS. Ah, all right.
I wouldn't be heard saying anything about one leg
I wouldn't say about the other.

PETER. Where
Did you get it, chum?

MEADOWS. I had it for my birthday.
Quite nice, isn't it? Five toes, it's got.

PETER. I mean where was the fighting, you wit?

MEADOWS [*jerking his head*]. Down the road.
My Uncle George had a thumping wooden leg,
Had it with him, on and off, for years.
When he gave up the world, it got out in the wash house.

DAVID. Has anybody thought what it's going to be like
Suppose we stay here for months or years?

ADAMS. Best they can do. You heard the towzer Commandant:
'All more buildings blow up into sky.
No place like home now. Roof here. Good and kind
To prisoners. Keep off sun, keep off rain.'

PETER. Keep off the grass.

DAVID. It's a festering idea for a prison camp.
You have to think twice every time you think,
In case what you think's a bit on the dubious side.
It's all this smell of cooped-up angels
Worries me.

PETER. What, us?

DAVID. Not mother's angels,
Dumb-cluck, God's angels.

PETER. Oh yes, them.
We're a worse fug to them, I shouldn't wonder.
We shall just have to make allowances.

DAVID. Beg pardon:
I'm talking to no-complaints Pete: arrangements perfect.

ADAMS. Too many pricking thistles in this straw:
Pricked to hell.

[PETER *has wandered across to the lectern.*

PETER. Note his early perpendicular
Language. Ecclesiastical influence.
See this? They've put us an English Bible.
There's careful nannies for you . . . 'These were the sons
Of Caleb the son of Hur, the firstborn of Ephratah:
Shobal the father of Kirjath-jearim, Salma
The father of Beth-lehem, Hareph the father
Of Beth-gader. And Shobal the father of Kirjath-
Jearim had sons: Haroeh, and half of the Manahethites——'
Interesting, isn't it?

DAVID. Stuff it, Pete.

PETER. 'And these were the sons of David, which were born unto Him in Hebron: the firstborn Amnon, of Ahinoam the

Jezreelitess: the second Daniel, of Abigail the
Carmelitess: the third Absalom the son of Maacah the
Daughter of Talmai king of Geshur: the fourth Adonijah
The son of Haggith: the fifth Shephatiah of Abital:
The sixth Ithream by Eglah his wife . . .'
Doing
All right, aren't you, Davey?

DAVID. So I did in Sunday school. You know what Absalom
Said to the tree? 'You're getting in my hair.'
And that's what I mean, so shut up.

PETER. Shut up we are.
Don't mind me. I'm making myself at home.
Now all I've got to do is try the pulpit.

ADAMS. Watch yourself, Pete. We've got years of this.

DAVID [*his temper growing*]. Any damn where he makes himself at home.
The world blows up, there's Pete there in the festering
Bomb-hole making cups of tea. I've had it
Week after week till I'm sick. Don't let's mind
What happens to anybody, don't let's object to anything,
Let's give the dirty towzers a cigarette,
There's nothing on earth worth getting warmed up about!
It doesn't matter who's on top, make yourself at home.

ADAMS. Character of Private Peter Able:
And not so far out at that. What we're in for
We've got to be in for and know just what it is.
Have some common sense, Pete. If you're looking for trouble
Go and have it in the vestry.

PETER [*up in the pulpit*]. How can I help it if I can't work myself up
About the way things go? It's a mystery to me.
We've had all this before. For God's sake

Be reasonable, Dave. Perhaps I was meant
To be a bishop.
[*He turns to the nave.*] Dearly beloved brothers
In a general muck-up, towzers included . . .

DAVID. What the hell do you think we're stuck here for
Locked in like lunatics? Just for a nice
New experience, with nice new friends
With nice new rifles to look after us?
We're at war with them, aren't we? And if we are
They're no blaming use!

PETER [*continuing to preach*]. We have here on my left
An example of the bestial passions that beset mankind.

[DAVID, *beside himself, leaps up the steps and attacks* PETER *in the pulpit.*

Davey, Dave . . . don't be a lunatic!

ADAMS. Come out of it,
King. Come down here, you great tomfool!

[*He goes to drag* DAVID *away.* DAVID *has his hands on* PETER'S *throat and has pushed him across the edge of the pulpit.*

DAVID [*raging*]. You laugh: I'll see you never laugh again.
Go on: laugh at this.

MEADOWS. If you don't get your hands away
You'll wish you never had 'em. Give over! Give over!

[DAVID *releases his hold. He pushes past* ADAMS *and comes down from the pulpit.*

I see the world in you very well. 'Tisn't
Your meaning, but you're a clumsy, wall-eyed bulldozer.
You don't know what you're hitting.

[DAVID *goes past him without a word, and throws himself on to his bed.*

Ah, well,
Neither do I, of course, come to that.

ADAMS. All right, Peter?

PETER. Think so, Corporal,
I'm not properly reassembled yet.
There's a bit of a rattle, but I think I had that before.

ADAMS. Dave had better damp down that filthy volcano
Or let me know what.

PETER. Oh, lord, I don't know,
It's who we happen to be. I suppose I'd better
Hit him back some time, or else he'll go mad
Trying to make me see daylight. I don't know.
I'll tell you my difficulty, Corp. I never remember
I ought to be fighting until I'm practically dead.
Sort of absent-fisted. Very worrying for Dave.

[*They have come down from the pulpit.* PETER *sways on his feet.* ADAMS *supports him.*

ADAMS. You're all in, Pete.

PETER. Say 'Fall out' and watch me
Fall.

ADAMS. All right, come on, we'll put you to bed.

[MEADOWS *has limped across with two blankets for* PETER'S *bunk.* DAVID *is watching anxiously.*

DAVID. What's wrong, Pete?

ADAMS. The best thing for you is keep
Out of this.

PETER. Dog-tired, that's all. It comes
Of taking orders. Dog collar too tight.

DAVID. I'll see to him.

ADAMS. I've seen you see to him.
Get back on your bed.

DAVID. I've never killed him yet.
I'm a pal of his.

ADAMS. That's right. I couldn't have expressed it
Better myself. We'll talk about that tomorrow.

[*He goes over to make up his own bunk.* DAVID *unlaces* PETER'*s boots.*

DAVID. How d'you feel now, Pete?

PETER. Beautiful.

DAVID. Why don't
You do some slaughtering sometimes? Why always
Leave it to me? Got no blood you can heat
Up or something? I didn't hurt you, did I,
Pete? How d'you feel?

PETER [*almost asleep*]. Um? Fine.

DAVID [*taking off* PETER'*s socks for him*]. The world's got to have us. Things go wrong.
We've got to finish the dirty towzers. It's been
A festering day, and I'm stinking tired. See you
Tomorrow.

[*He leaves* PETER *sleeping, goes over to his own bunk, and throws himself down.*

ADAMS [*to* MEADOWS]. I sometimes feel a bit like Dave
Myself, about Pete. You have to tell him there's a war on.

[MEADOWS *has taken his boots and socks off and is lying on top of his blankets.*

MEADOWS. Sometimes I think if it wasn't for the words, Corporal,
I should be very given to talking. There's things
To be said which would surprise us if ever we said them.

ADAMS. Don't give us any more surprises, for God's sake.

MEADOWS. There's things would surprise us.

ADAMS [*studying the sole of his foot*]. Like the size of that blister.

MEADOWS. Or even bigger. Well, good night, Corporal.

ADAMS. G'night, boy.

MEADOWS. I'm old enough to be
Your father.

ADAMS. I thought you might be. How did you get
Pulled in on this?

MEADOWS. I thought I would.
I got in under the fence. Not a soul
At the War Office had noticed me being born.
I'd only my mother's word for it myself,
And she never knew whether it was Monday washing-day
Or Thursday baking-day. She only knew
I made it hindering awkward.

ADAMS. Are you glad
You came?

MEADOWS. Ah, now. Well,
Glad, yes, and sorry, yes, and so as that.
I remember how it came over me, as I
Was dunging a marrow bed. Tim, I said to me—
'Cos being a widower I do the old lady's
Talking for her, since she fell silent—Tim,
You're in the way to curse. Thinking of the enemy
And so as that. And I cursed up and about.
But cursing never made anything for a man yet.

So having had the pleasure of it, I came along
To take a hand. But there's strange divisions in us,
And in every man, one side or the other.
When I'm not too good I hear myself talking away
Like Tim Meadows M.P., at the other end of my head.
Sounds all right. I'd like to know what I say.
Might be interesting.

ADAMS. I shouldn't worry.
I'm going to take a last look at Pete.
G'night, boy.

MEADOWS [*already almost asleep*]. Hope so.

[ADAMS *goes over to* PETER'*s bunk.*

DAVID. Corp.

ADAMS. Hullo.

DAVID. How long are we here for?

ADAMS. A million years.
So you'd better get to like it.

DAVID. Give us
Cassock and surplice drill tomorrow, Joe.

ADAMS. O.K. Wash your feet.

DAVID. How's Pete? Asleep?

ADAMS. Couldn't be more if he died.

DAVID [*starting up on his elbow*]. What do you mean?

ADAMS. I mean he's breathing like an easy conscience. Why don't you
Get down to it yourself? There's tomorrow to come,
According to orders. Good night, King of Israel.

DAVID. Oh, go
And discard yourself. G'night, Corporal Joseph Adams.

[ADAMS *goes to his bunk.* MEADOWS *turns in his sleep. The church clock strikes a single note.*

MEADOWS [*asleep*]. Who's that, fallen out? How many men?
How many? I said only one.
One was enough.
No, no, no. I didn't ask to be God.
No one else prepared to spell the words.
Spellbound. B-o-u-n-d. Ah-h-h-h . . .

[*He turns in his sleep again.*

It's old Adam, old, old, old Adam.
Out of bounds. No one said fall out.
What time did you go to bad?
Sorrow, Adam, stremely sorrow.

[CORPORAL ADAMS *comes towards him, a dream figure.*

Adam, Adam, stand easy there.

ADAMS. Reporting for duty, sir.

MEADOWS. As you were, Adam.

ADAMS. No chance of that, sir.

MEADOWS. As you were, as you were.

ADAMS. Lost all track of it now, sir.

MEADOWS. How far back was it, Adam?

ADAMS [*with a jerk of the head*]. Down the road. Too dark to see.

MEADOWS. Were you alone?

ADAMS. A woman with me, sir.

MEADOWS. I said Let there be love,
And there wasn't enough light, you say?

ADAMS. We could see our own shapes, near enough,
But not the road. The road kept on dividing
Every yard or so. Makes it long.
We expected nothing like it, sir.
Ill-equipped, naked as the day,
It was all over and the world was on us
Before we had time to take cover.

MEADOWS. Stand at peace, Adam: do stand at peace.

ADAMS. There's nothing of that now, sir.

MEADOWS. Corporal Adam.

ADAMS. Sir?

MEADOWS. You have shown spirit.

ADAMS. Thank you, sir.
Excuse me, sir, but there's some talk of a future.
I've had no instructions.

MEADOWS [*turning in his sleep*]. Ah-h-h-h-h.

ADAMS. Is there any immediate anxiety of that?

[DAVID, *as the dream figure of Cain, stands leaning on the lectern, chewing at a beet.*

How far can we fall back, sir?

DAVID [*smearing his arms with beet juice*]. Have you lost something?

ADAMS. Yes, Cain: yes, I have.

DAVID. Have you felt in all your pockets?

ADAMS. Yes, and by searchlight all along the grass
For God knows howling. Not a sign,
Not a sign, boy, not a ghost.

DAVID. When do you last
Remember losing it?

ADAMS. When I knew it was mine.
As soon as I knew it was mine I felt
I was the only one who didn't know
My host.

DAVID. Poor overlooked
Old man. Allow me to make the introduction.
God: man. Man: God.

[PETER, *the dream figure of Abel, is in the organ-loft fingering out 'Now the day is over'.*

ADAMS. I wish it could be so easy.

DAVID. Sigh, sigh, sigh!
The hot sun won't bring you out again
If you don't know how to behave.
Pretty much like mutiny. I'd like to remind you
We're first of all men, and complain afterwards.
[*Calling.*] Abel! Abel! Hey, flock-headed Peter,
Come down off those mountains.
Those bleating sheep can look after themselves.
Come on down.

PETER. What for?

DAVID. Because I said so!

PETER [*coming down*]. I overlooked the time. Is it day or night?

DAVID. You don't deserve to inherit the earth.
Am I supposed to carry the place alone?

PETER. Where will you carry it?
Where do you think you're going to take it to,
This prolific indifference?
Show me an ending great enough
To hold the passion of this beginning
And raise me to it.

Day and night, the sun and moon
Spirit us, we wonder where. Meanwhile
Here we are, we lean on our lives
Expecting purpose to keep her date,
Get cold waiting, watch the overworlds
Come and go, question the need to stay
But do, in an obstinate anticipation of love.
Ah, love me, it's a long misuse of breath
For boys like us. When do we start?

DAVID. When you suffering god'sbodies
Come to your senses. What you'll do
Is lose us life altogether.
Amply the animal is Cain, thank God,
As he was meant to be: a huskular strapling
With all his passions about him. Tomorrow
Will know him well. Momentous doings
Over the hill for the earth and us.
What hell else do you want?

PETER. The justification.

DAVID. Oh, bulls and bears to that.
The word's too long to be lived.
Just if, just if, is as far as ever you'll see.

PETER. What's man to be?

DAVID. Content and full.

PETER. That's modest enough.
What an occupation for eternity.
Sky's hollow filled as far as for ever
With rolling light: place without limit,
Time without pity:
And did you say all for the sake of our good condition,
All for our two-footed prosperity?

Well, we should prosper, considering
The torment squandered on our prospering.
From squid to eagle the ravening is on.
We are all pain-fellows, but nothing you dismay,
Man is to prosper. Other lives, forbear
To blame me, great and small forgive me
If to your various agonies
My light should seem hardly enough
To be the cause of the ponderable shadow.

DAVID. Who do you think you are, so Angel-sick?
Pain warns us to be master: pain prefers us.
Draws us up.

PETER. Water into the sun:
All the brooding clouds of us!

DAVID. All right.
We'll put it to the High and Mighty.
Play you dice to know who's favoured.

PETER. What's he to do with winning?

DAVID. Play you dice.
Not so sure of yourself, I notice.

PETER. I'll play you. Throw for first throw.
Now creation be true to creatures.

ADAMS. Look, sir, my sons are playing.
How silent the spectators are,
World, air, and water.
Eyes bright, tension, halt.
Still as a bone from here to the sea.

DAVID [*playing*]. Ah-h-h-h!

ADAMS. Sir, my sons are playing. Cain's your man.
He goes in the mould of passion as you made him.
He can walk this broken world as easily
As I and Eve the ivory light of Eden.
I recommend him. The other boy
Frets for what never came his way,
Will never reconcile us to our exile.
Look, sir, my sons are playing.
Sir, let the future plume itself, not suffer.

PETER [*playing*]. How's that for a nest of singing birds?

ADAMS. Cain sweats: Cain gleams. Now do you see him?
He gives his body to the game.
Sir, he's your own making, and has no complaints.

DAVID. Ah! What are you doing to me, heaven and earth?

PETER. Friendly morning.

DAVID [*shaking the dice*]. Numbers, be true to nature.
Deal me high,
Six dark stars
Come into my sky.

[*He throws.*

Blight! What's blinding me
By twos and threes? I'm strong, aren't I?
Who's holding me down? Who's frozen my fist
So it can't hatch the damn dice out?

PETER [*shaking and throwing*].
Deal me high, deal me low.
Make my deeds
My nameless needs.
I know I do not know.
. . . That brings me home!

[DAVID *roars with rage and disappointment.*

DAVID. Life is a hypocrite if I can't live
The way it moves me! I was trusted
Into breath. Why am I doubted now?
Flesh is my birthplace. Why shouldn't I speak the tongue?
What's the disguise, eh? Who's the lurcher
First enjoys us, then disowns us?
Keep me clean of God, creation's crooked.

ADAMS. Cain, steady, steady, you'll raise the world.

DAVID. You bet your roots I will.
I'll know what game of hide and seek this is.
Half and half, my petering brother says,
Nothing of either, in and out the limbo.
'I know I do not know' he says.
So any lion can BE, and any ass,
And any cockatoo: and all the unbiddable
Roaming voices up and down
Can live their lives and welcome
While I go pestered and wondering down hill
Like a half-wit angel strapped to the back of a mule.
Thanks! I'll be as the body was first presumed.

PETER. It was a game between us, Cain.

DAVID [*in a fury*]. Your dice were weighted! You thought you could trick
The life out of me. We'll see about that.
You think you're better than you're created!
I saw the smiles that went between
You and the top air. I knew your game.
Look helpless, let him see you're lost,
Make him amiable to think
He made more strangely than he thought he did!
Get out of time, will you, get out of time!

[*He takes* PETER *by the throat.* ADAMS *goes to part them.*

ADAMS. Cain, drop those hands!

[He is wheeled by an unknown force back against his bunk.

O Sir,
Let me come to them. They're both
Out of my reach. I have to separate them.

DAVID [*strangling* PETER]. You leave us now, leave us, you half-and-half:
I want to be free of you!

PETER. Cain! Cain!

ADAMS. Cain, Cain!

DAVID. If life's not good enough for you
Go and justify yourself!

ADAMS. Pinioned here, when out of my body
I made them both, the fury and the suffering,
The fury, the suffering, the two ways
Which here spreadeagle me.

[DAVID *has fought* PETER *back to the bed and kills him.*

O, O, O,
Eve, what love there was between us. Eve,
What gentle thing, a son, so harmless,
Can hang the world with blood.

DAVID [*to* PETER]. Oh,
You trouble me. You are dead.

ADAMS. How ceaseless the earth is. How it goes on.
Nothing has happened except silence where sound was,
Stillness where movement was. Nothing has happened,
But the future is like a great pit.
My heart breaks, quiet as petals falling
One by one, but this is the drift
Of agony for ever.

DAVID. Now let's hope
There will be no more argument,
No more half-and-half, no more doubt,
No more betrayal.—You trouble me,
You trouble me.

MEADOWS [*in his sleep*]. Cain.

[DAVID *hides*

Cain. Where is
Your brother?

DAVID. How should I know? Am I
His keeper?

ADAMS. Where is keeping?
Keep somewhere, world, the time we love.
I have two sons, and where is one,
And where will now the other be?
I am a father unequipped to save.
When I was young the trees of love forgave me:
That was all. But now they say
The days of such simple forgiveness are done,
Old Joe Adam all sin and bone.

MEADOWS. Cain: I hear your brother's blood
Crying to me from the ground.

DAVID. Sir, no: he is silent.
All the crying is mine.

MEADOWS. Run, run, run. Cain
Is after you.

DAVID. What shall I do?

MEADOWS. What you have done. It does it to you.
Nowhere rest. Cage of the world
Holds your prowling. Howl, Cain, jackal afraid.

And nowhere, Cain, nowhere
Escape the fear of what men fear in you.
Every man's hand will be against you,
But never touch you into quietness.
Run! Run!

DAVID. The punishment
Is more than I can bear. I loved life
With a good rage you gave me. And how much better
Did Abel do? He set up his heart
Against your government of flesh.
How was I expected to guess
That what I am you didn't want?
God the jailer, God the gun
Watches me exercise in the yard,
And all good neighbourhood has gone.
The two-faced beater makes me fly,
Fair game, poor game, damned game
For God and all man-hunters.

MEADOWS. They shall never kill you.

DAVID. Death was a big word, and now it has come
An act so small, my enemies will do it
Between two jobs. Cain's alive,
Cain's dead, we'll carry the bottom field:
Killing is light work, and Cain is easily dead.

MEADOWS. Run on, keep your head down, cross at the double
The bursts of open day between the nights.
My word is Bring him in alive.
Can you feel it carved on your body?

[DAVID *twists as though he felt a branding iron touch him.*

DAVID. God in heaven! The drag!
You're tearing me out of my life still living!

This can't last on flesh for ever.
Let me sleep, let me, let me, let me sleep.
God, let me sleep. God, let me sleep.

[*He goes into the shadows to his bed.*

MEADOWS [*turning in bed*]. This can't last on flesh for ever.
Let me sleep.

[*There follows a pause of heavy breathing. The church clock in the tower strikes the three-quarters.* MEADOWS *wakes, props himself up on his elbow.*

Any of you boys awake?
Takes a bit of getting used to, sleeping
In a looming great church. How you doing?
I can't rest easy for the night of me.
. . . Sleeping like great roots, every Jack of them.
How many draughts are sifting under the doors.
Pwhee-ooo. And the breathing: and breathing: heavy and deep:
Breathing: heavy and deep.
Sighing the life out of you. All the night.

[DAVID *stirs uneasily.*

DAVID. I don't have to stay here! I'm a King.

MEADOWS. David, that you? You awake, David?
A dream's dreaming him. This is no place
For lying awake. When other men are asleep
A waking man's a lost one. Tim, go byes.

[*He covers his head with his blanket.*

DAVID [*in his sleep*]. I'm King of Israel. They told me so.
I'm doing all right. But who is there to trust?
There are so many fools. Fools and fools and fools,
All round my throne. Loved and alone
David keeps the earth. And nothing kills them.

[PETER, *as the dream figure of Absalom, stands with his back pressed against a wall as though afraid to be seen.*

PETER. Do you think I care?

DAVID. Who is that man down there
In the dark alley-way making mischief?

PETER. Do you think I care?

DAVID. Corporal Joab:
There's a man in the dark way. Do you see
That shadow shift? it has a belly and ribs.
It's a man, Joab, who shadows me. He lurks
Against my evening temper. Dangerous.

[ADAMS *appears as the dream figure of Joab.*

ADAMS. I think you know already.

DAVID. He has got to be named. Which of us does it?

ADAMS. He's your own son: Absalom.

DAVID. Now
The nightmare sits and eats with me.
He was boy enough.
Why does he look like a thief?

ADAMS. Because
He steals your good, he steals your strength,
He riddles your world until it sinks,
He plays away all your security,
All you labour and suffer to hold
Against the enemy.

DAVID. The world's back
Is bent and heavily burdened, and yet he thinks
He can leapfrog over. Absalom,
Absalom, why do you play the fool against me?

PETER. You and your enemies! Everlastingly
Thinking of enemies. Open up.
Your enemies are friends of mine.

DAVID. They gather against our safety. They make trash
Of what is precious to us. Absalom,
Come over here. I want to speak to you.

PETER [*running up into the pulpit*]. Do you think I care?

ADAMS. If you let him run
He'll make disaster certain.

DAVID. Absalom,
Come alive. Living is caring.
Hell is making straight towards us.

PETER [*in the pulpit*]. Beloved, all who pipe your breath
Under the salted almond moon,
Hell is in my father's head
Making straight towards him. Please forget it.
He sees the scarlet shoots of spring
And thinks of blood. He sees the air
Streaming with imagined hordes
And conjures them to come. But you and I
Know that we can turn away
And everything will turn
Into itself again. What is
A little evil here and there between friends?
Shake hands on it: shake hands, shake hands:
Have a cigarette, and make yourselves at home.
Shall we say what we think of the King of Israel?
Ha—ha—ha!

[*Jeering laughter echoes round the roof of the church.*

DAVID. Don't do it to me, don't make the black rage
Shake me, Peter. I tremble like an earthquake
Because I can't find words which might
Put the fear of man into you.
Understand! The indecisions
Have to be decided. Who's against us
Reeks to God. Where's your hand?
Be ordinary human, Absalom.

ADAMS. Appeal's no use, King. He has
A foiling heart: the sharp world glances off
And so he's dangerous.

DAVID. I think so too.
Who can put eyes in his head? Who'll do it,
Eh, Joab? We have to show him
This terse world means business, don't we, Corporal,
Don't we?

ADAMS. He has to be instructed.

DAVID. Make a soldier of him. Make him fit
For conflict, as the stars and stags are.
He belongs to no element now. We have
To have him with us. Show him the way,
Joe Adams.

[PETER *is lounging at the foot of the pulpit.* ADAMS *turns to him.*

ADAMS. Get on parade.

PETER. What's the music?

ADAMS. I'll sing you, Absalom, if you don't get moving.
And I'll see you singing where you never meant.
Square up.

PETER. What's this?

ADAMS. Square up, I said.

PETER. Where do we go from here?

ADAMS. It's unarmed combat.
It's how your bare body makes them die.
It's old hey-presto death: you learn the trick
And death's the rabbit out of the hat:
Rolling oblivion for someone.
You've got to know how to get rid of the rats of the world.
They're up at your throat. Come on.

PETER. What nightmare's this you're dragging me into?

ADAMS. Humanity's. Come on.

PETER. I know
Nothing about it. Life's all right to me.

ADAMS. Say that when it comes.

[*The unarmed combat*, ADAMS *instructing*.

DAVID. Where is he going now? He carries
No light with him. Does he know
The river's unbound: it's up above
Every known flood-mark, and still rising.

PETER [*who has got away from* ADAMS]. I'm on the other side of the river
Staying with friends, whoever they are.
Showery still, but I manage to get out,
I manage to get out.
The window marked with a cross is where I sleep.
Just off to a picnic with your enemies.
They're not bad fellows, once you get to know them.

DAVID [*to* ADAMS]. I have heard from my son.

ADAMS. What's his news?

DAVID. He's with the enemy. He betrays us, Joab.
He has to be counted with them.
Are we ready?

ADAMS. Only waiting for the word.

DAVID. We attack at noon.

ADAMS. Only hoping for the time.
Good luck.

DAVID. Good luck.

[ADAMS *walks down the chancel steps and crouches, keeping a steady eye on his wrist-watch.* ADAMS *gives a piercing whistle.* PETER *leaps up and hangs on to the edge of the pulpit.* ADAMS *cuts him down with a tommy-gun. He cries out.* DAVID *starts up in his bunk.* PETER *and* ADAMS *fall to the floor and lie prone.*

[*Awake.*] What's the matter, Peter? Pete! Anything wrong?

[*He gets out of his bunk and goes across to Peter's.*

Pete, are you awake?

[*He stands for a moment and then recrosses the floor.*

MEADOWS [*awake*]. Anything the matter?
Can't you sleep either?

DAVID [*getting back into his bunk*]. I thought I heard
Somebody shout. It woke me up.

MEADOWS. Nobody shouted.
I've been lying awake. It's just gone midnight.
There's a howling wind outside plays ducks and drakes
With a flat moon: just see it through this window:
It flips across the clouds and then goes under:
I wish I could run my head against some sleep.

This building's big for lying with your eyes open.
You could brush me off, and only think you're dusting.
Who's got the key of the crypt? [*He yawns.*]
Thanks for waking. It brings the population
Up to two. You're a silent chap. Dave?
Have you gone to sleep again already?
Back into the sea, like a slippery seal.
And here am I, high and dry.

DAVID [*asleep*]. Look, look, look.

MEADOWS. Away he goes,
Drifting far out. How much of him is left?
Ah, lord, man, go to sleep: stop worrying.

[ADAMS *drags or carries* PETER *to Peter's bunk.*

DAVID. Joab, is that you? Joab, is that you?
What are you bringing back?

ADAMS. The victory.

DAVID. Are you sure it is the victory, Joab?
Are we ever sure it's the victory?
So many times you've come back, Joab,
With something else. I want to be sure at last.
I want to know what you mean by victory.
Is it something else to me? Where are you looking?
There's nothing that way. But look over here:
There's something. Along the road, starting the dust,
He wants to reach us. Why is that?
So you're going to walk away.

ADAMS [*going to his bunk*]. I've done my best.
I can't be held responsible for everything.

DAVID. Don't leave me, Joab. Stay and listen.

ADAMS [*covering himself over*]. I'm dead beat.
The enemy's put to flight. Good night, you King of Israel.

DAVID. Bathed in sweat, white with dust. Call him here.
Come up. I am the King.
I shall wait patiently until your voice
Gets back the breath to hit me. I'm here, waiting.

[DAVID *sits on the edge of his bunk, a red army blanket hanging from his shoulder.*

MEADOWS [*awake*]. Where are you off to, Davey?
Get you back to bed. A dream
Has got you prisoner, Davey, like
The world has got us all. Don't let it
Take you in.

DAVID. Come here to me, come over
Here, the dusty fellow with the news,
Come here. Is the fighting over? Unconditionally?

[MEADOWS *has left his bunk and crossed to* DAVID.

MEADOWS. Lie down, boy. Forget it. It's all over.

DAVID. Is the young man Absalom safe?

MEADOWS Lie down, Dave.
Everybody's asleep.

ADAMS [*from his bunk*]. The boy's dead.
You might as well be told: I say
The boy's dead.

[DAVID, *giving a groan, lies back on his bed.*

MEADOWS. The night's over us.
Nothing's doing. Except the next day's in us
And makes a difficult sort of lying-in.
Here, let's cover you up. Keep the day out of this.
Find something better to sleep about.

Give your living heart a rest. Do you hear me,
Dave, down where you are? If you don't mind,
While I'm here, I'll borrow some of that sleep:
You've got enough for two.

[*He limps back to his bunk, passing* ADAMS, *who wakes.*

ADAMS. Hullo, Meadows:
What's worrying you?

MEADOWS. Dave was. He couldn't
Let go of the day. He started getting up
And walking in his sleep.

ADAMS. All right now?

MEADOWS. Seems running smoother.

ADAMS. Is that him talking?

[PETER *has begun to talk in his sleep.*

MEADOWS. Muttering monkeys love us, it's the other one now:
Peter's at it.

PETER. Do I have to follow you?

ADAMS. You needn't hear him if you get your ears
Under the blankets. That's where I'm going.
Good-night, boy.

[*He disappears under his blankets.* MEADOWS *climbs into his bunk.*

MEADOWS. Hope so. It's a choppy crossing
We're having still. No coast of daylight yet for miles.

[*He also disappears from view. A pause. The church clock strikes midnight.*

PETER [*asleep*]. Why did you call me? I'm contented here:
They say I'm in a prison. Morning comes
To a prison like a nurse.

A rustling presence, as though a small breeze came,
And presently a voice. I think
We're going to live. The dark pain has gone,
The relief of daylight
Flows over me, as though beginning is
Beginning. The hills roll in and make their homes,
And gradually unfold the plains. Breath
And light are cool together now.
The earth is all transparent, but too deep
To see down to its bed.

[DAVID, *the dream figure of Abraham, stands beside* PETER.

DAVID. Come with me.

PETER. Where are we going?

DAVID. If necessary
To break our hearts. It's as well for the world.

PETER. There's enough breaking, God knows. We die,
And the great cities come down like avalanches.

DAVID. But men come down like living men.
Time gives the promise of time in every death,
Not of any ceasing. Come with me.
The cities are pitifully concerned.
We need to go to the hill.

PETER. What shall we do?

DAVID. What falls to us.

PETER. Falling from where?

DAVID. From the point of devotion, meaning God.
Carry this wood, Isaac, and this coil
Of rope.

PETER. I'm coming.

DAVID. There has to be sacrifice.
I know that. There's nothing so sure.

PETER. You walk so fast. These things are heavy.

DAVID. I know. I carry them too.

PETER. I only want
To look around a bit. There's so much to see.
Ah, peace on earth, I'm a boy for the sights.

DAVID. Don't break my heart. You so
Cling hold of the light. I have to take it
All away.

PETER. Why are you so grave?
There's more light than we can hold. Everything
Grows over with fresh inclination
Every day. You and I are both
Immeasurably living.

[DAVID *has been walking towards the pulpit.* PETER *still lies in bed. He starts to whistle a tune, though the whistling seems not to come from his lips but from above him.*

DAVID. What do you whistle for?

PETER. I whistle for myself
And anyone who likes it.

DAVID. Keep close to me.
It may not be for long. Time huddles round us,
A little place to be in. And we're already
Up the heavy hill. The singing birds
Drop down and down to the bed of the trees,
To the hay-silver evening, O
Lying gentleness, a thin veil over
The long scars from the nails of the warring hearts.

Come up, son, and see the world.
God dips his hand in death to wash the wound,
Takes evil to inoculate our lives
Against infectious evil. We'll go on.
I am history's wish and must come true,
And I shall hate so long as hate
Is history, though, God, it drives
My life away like a beaten dog. Here
Is the stone where we have to sacrifice.
Make my heart like it. It still is beating
Unhappily the human time.

PETER. Where is the creature that has to die?
There's nothing here of any life worth taking.
Shall we go down again?

DAVID. There is life here.

PETER. A flinching snail, a few unhopeful harebells.
What good can they be?

DAVID. What else?

PETER. You, father,
And me.

DAVID. I know you're with me. But very strangely
I stand alone with a knife. For the simple asking.
Noon imperial will no more let me keep you
Than if you were the morning dew. The day
Wears on. Shadows of our history
Steal across the sky. For our better freedom
Which makes us living men: for what will be
The heaven on earth, I have to bind you
With cords, and lay you here on the stone's table.

PETER. Are you going to kill me? No! Father!
I've come only a short way into life
And I can see great distance waiting.
The free and evening air
Swans from hill to hill.
Surely there's no need for us to be
The prisoners of the dark? Smile, father.
Let me go.

DAVID. Against my heart
I let you go, for the world's own ends
I let you go, for God's will
I let you go, for children's children's joy
I let you go, my grief obeying.
The cords bind you against my will
But you're bound for a better world.
And I must lay you down to sleep
For a better waking. Come now.

[*In mime he picks Isaac up in his arms and lays him across the front of the pulpit.*

PETER [*in his bunk*]. I'm afraid.
And how is the earth going to answer, even so?

DAVID. As it will. How can we know?
But we must do, and the future make amends.

PETER. Use the knife quickly. There are too many
Thoughts of life coming to the cry.
God put them down until I go.
Now, now, suddenly!

DAVID [*the knife raised*]. This
Cuts down my heart, but bitter events must be.

I can't learn to forgive necessity:
God help me to forgive it.

[ADAMS *appears as the dream figure of the Angel.*

ADAMS. Hold your arm.
There are new instructions. The knife can drop
Harmless and shining.

DAVID. I never thought to know,
Strange voice of mercy, such happy descending.
Nor my son again. But he's here untouched,
And evening is at hand
As clear and still as no man.

PETER. Father, I feel
The air go over me as though I should live.

DAVID. So you will, for the earth's while. Shall I
Undo the cords?

ADAMS. These particular. But never all.
There's no loosening, since men with men
Are like the knotted sea. Lift him down
From the stone to the grass again, and, even so free,
Yet he will find the angry cities hold him.
But let him come back to the strange matter of living
As best he can: and take instead
The ram caught here by the white wool
In the barbed wire of the briar bush:
Make that the kill of the day.

DAVID. Readily.

PETER. Between the day and the night
The stars tremble in balance.
The houses are beginning to come to light.
And so it would have been if the knife had killed me.

This would have been my death-time.
The ram goes in my place, in a curious changing.
Chance, as fine as a thread,
Cares to keep me, and I go my way.

MEADOWS [*a dream figure*]. Do you want a ride across the sands,
Master Isaac?

PETER. Who are you?

MEADOWS. Now, boy, boy,
Don't make a joke of me. Old Meadows,
The donkey man, who brought you up the hill.
Not remember me? That's a man's memory,
Short measure as that. Down a day.
And we've been waiting, Edwina and me,
As patient as two stale loaves, to take you down.

PETER. But I climbed the hill on foot.

MEADOWS [*patting the bunk*]. No credit, Edwina girl, no credit.
He thinks you're a mangy old moke. You tell him
There's none so mangy as thinks that others are.
You have it for the sake of the world.

PETER. All right, she can take me down. I'm rasping tired.
My whole body's like a three days' growth of beard.
But I don't know why she should have to carry me.
She's nothing herself but two swimming eyes
And a cask of ribs.

MEADOWS. A back's a back.
She's as good as gold while she lives,
And after that she's as good as dead. Where else
Would you find such a satisfactory soul?
Gee-up, you old millennium. She's slow,
But it's kind of onwards. Jog, jog,
Jog, jog.

PETER. There's a ram less in the world tonight.
My heart, I could see, was thudding in its eyes.
It was caught, and now it's dead.

MEADOWS. Jog, jog,
Jog, jog, jog, jog, jog,
Jog, jog.

PETER. Across the sands and into the sea.
The sun flocks along the waves.
Blowing up for rain of sand.
Helter-shelter.

MEADOWS. Jog. Jog. Jog.
Donkey ride is over. In under
The salty planks and corrugated iron.
Stable for mangy mokes. Home, old girl,
Home from the sea, old Millie-edwinium.
Tie up here.

[He has climbed into his bunk.

PETER. No eyes open. All
In sleep. The innocence has come.
Ram's wool hill pillow is hard.

[He sighs and turns in his bunk. The church clock strikes one. An aeroplane is heard flying over the church. PETER *wakens and sits up in his bunk, listening.*

Is that one of ours?

MEADOWS *[his face emerging from the blankets].*
Just tell me: are you awake
Or asleep?

PETER. Awake. Listen. Do you hear it?
Is it one of ours?

MEADOWS. No question: one of ours.
Or one of theirs.

PETER. Gone over. Funny question:
'Was I asleep?' when I was sitting up
Asking you a question.

MEADOWS. Dave's been sitting up
Asking questions, as fast asleep as an old dog.
And you've been chatting away like old knitting-needles,
Half the night.

PETER. What was I saying?

MEADOWS. I know all
Your secrets now, man.

PETER. I wish I did.
What did I say?

MEADOWS. Like the perfect gentleman
I obliterated my lug-holes:
Under two blankets, army issue.
A man must be let to have a soul to himself
Or souls will go the way of tails.
I wouldn't blame a man for sleeping.
It comes to some. To others it doesn't come.
Troubles differ. But I should be glad
To stop lying out here in the open
While you underearthly lads
Are shut away talking night's language like natives.
We only have to have Corporal Adams
To make a start, and I might as well
Give up the whole idea. Oh, lord, let me
Race him to it. I'm going under now
For the third time.

[*He covers his head with the blankets.*

PETER. Sorry if I disturbed you.
I'll go back where I came from, and if I can
I'll keep it to myself. Poor old Meadows:
Try thinking of love, or something.
Amor vincit insomnia.

MEADOWS. That's enough
Of night classes. What's it mean?

PETER. The writing on the wall. So turn
Your face to it: get snoring.

MEADOWS. Not hereabouts:
It wouldn't be reverent. Good night, then.

PETER. Same to you.

[*They cover their heads. A pause.* ADAMS, *asleep, lies flat on his bunk, looking down over the foot of it.*

ADAMS. Fish, fish, fish in the sea, you flash
Through your clouds of water like the war in heaven:
Angel-fish and swordfish, the silver troops . . .
And I am salt and sick on a raft above you,
Wondering for land, but there's no homeward
I can see.

[*He turns on his back.*

God, have mercy
On our sick shoals, darting and dying.
We're strange fish to you. How long
Can you drift over our sea, and not give up
The ghost of hope? The air is bright between us.
The flying fish make occasional rainbows,
But land, your land and mine, is nowhere yet.

[DAVID, *a dream figure, comes to meet him.*

How can a man learn navigation
When there's no rudder? You can seem to walk,
You there: you can seem to walk:
But presently you drown.

DAVID. Who wants us, Corporal?

ADAMS. I wish I knew. I'm soaked to the skin.
The world shines wet. I think it's men's eyes everywhere
Reflecting light. Presently you drown.

DAVID. Have you forgotten you're a prisoner?
They marched us thirty miles in the pouring rain.
Remember that? They, they, they, they.

[PETER *comes down towards* DAVID, *marching but exhausted. As he reaches* DAVID *he reels and* DAVID *catches him.*

PETER. What happens if I fall out, Dave?

DAVID. You don't fall out, that's all.

PETER. They can shoot me if they like.
It'll be a bit of a rest.

DAVID. You're doing all right.

PETER. I wouldn't know. It. Feels.
Damned. Odd. To me.

DAVID. Corporal Adams,
Man half-seas overboard!
Can you lend a hand?

ADAMS [*jumping from his bunk*]. Here I come.
Does he want to be the little ghost?
Give us an arm. Dave and I will be
Your anchor, boy: keep you from drifting
Away where you're not wanted yet.

PETER. Don't think you've got me with you.
I dropped out miles ago.

ADAMS. We'll keep the memory green.

[*They do not move forward, but seem to be trudging.*

DAVID. They, they, they, they.

ADAMS. Be careful how you step. These logs we're on
Are slimy and keep moving apart.

DAVID [*breaking away*]. Where do you think we are?
We're prisoners, God! They've bricked us in.

ADAMS. Who said you were dismissed?

PETER. Forget your stripes
For a minute, Corporal: it's my birthday next month,
My birthday, Corporal: into the world I came,
The barest chance it happened to be me,
The naked truth of all that led the way
To make me. I'm going for a stroll.

[*He wanders down towards the lectern.*

ADAMS. Where are you going? Orders are
No man leaves unless in a state of death.

DAVID. There's nowhere to go, and he knows
There's nowhere to go. He's trying to pretend
We needn't be here.

PETER. Don't throttle yourself
With swallowing, Dave. Anyone
Would think you never expected the world.
Listen to the scriptures:
[*As though reading the Bible.*]
Nebuchadnezzar, hitting the news,
Made every poor soul lick his shoes.

When the shoes began to wear
Nebuchadnezzar fell back on prayer.
Here endeth the first lesson. And here beginneth
The second lesson . . .

DAVID. I'll read the second lesson:
God drown you for a rat, and let the world
Go down without you.

PETER. Three blind mice of Gotham,
Shadrac, Meshac and Abednego:
They went to walk in a fire.
If the fire had been hotter
Their tales would have been shorter.
Here endeth——

ADAMS. Get into the ranks.

PETER. What's worrying you? We're not
On active service now. Maybe it's what
They call in our paybooks 'disembodied service':
So drill my spirit, Corporal, till it weeps
For mercy everywhere.

DAVID. It had better weep,
It had better weep. By God, I'll say
We have to be more than men if we're to man
This rising day. They've been keeping from us
Who we are, till now, when it's too late
To recollect. [*Indicating* PETER.] Does he know?

ADAMS. Shadrac, Meshac, Abednego—
We didn't have those names before: I'll swear
We were at sea. This black morning
Christens us with names that were never ours
And makes us pay for them. Named,

Condemned. What they like to call us
Matters more than anything at heart.
Hearts are here to stop
And better if they do. God help us all.

PETER. Do I know what?

ADAMS. We are your three blind mice:
Our names are Shadrac, Meshac, and Abednego.
This is our last morning. Who knows truly
What that means, except us?

PETER. And which of us
Knows truly? O God in heaven, we're bound
To wake up out of this. Wake, wake, wake:
This is not my world! Where have you brought me?

DAVID. To feed what you've been riding pick-a-back.

PETER. I can believe anything, except
The monster.

DAVID. And the monster's here.

ADAMS. To make
Sure we know eternity's in earnest.

PETER. It's here to kill. What's that in earnest of?
But the world comes up even over the monster's back.
Corporal, can we make a dash for the hill there?

ADAMS. We're under close arrest.

DAVID. O God, are we
To be shut up here in what other men do
And watch ourselves be ground and battered
Into their sins? Let me, dear God, be active
And seem to do right, whatever damned result.
Let me have some part in what goes on
Or I shall go mad!

PETER. What's coming now
Their eyes are on us. Do you see them?

ADAMS. Inspection. The powers have come to look us over
To see if we're in fettle for the end.
Get into line.

DAVID. What, for those devils?
Who are they?

ADAMS. Nebuchadnezzar and his aides.
Do what you're told.

PETER. Is that him with one eye?

DAVID. Are they ours or theirs?

ADAMS. Who are we, Dave, who
Are we? If we could get the hang of that
We might know what side they're on. I should say
On all sides. Which is why the open air
Feels like a barrack square.

PETER. Is that him
With one eye?

ADAMS. If we could know who we are——

DAVID. I've got to know which side I'm on.
I've got to be on a side.

ADAMS. —They're coming up.
Let's see you jump to it this time: we're coming
Up for the jump. We can't help it if
We hate his guts.—Look out.—Party, shun!

[*They all come to attention.*

The three prisoners, sir.—Party, stand
At ease!

PETER. Purple and stars and red and gold.
What are they celebrating?

DAVID. We shall know soon.

ADAMS. Stop talking in the ranks.

[*They stand silent for a moment.*

PETER. What bastard language
Is he talking? Are we supposed to guess?
Police on earth. Aggression is the better
Part of Allah. Liberating very high
The dying and the dead. Freedoom, freedoom.
Will he never clear his throat?

DAVID. He's moving on

ADAMS. Party, at-ten-tion!

[*They bring their heels together, but they cannot bring their hands from behind their backs.*

PETER. Corporal, our hands are tied!

DAVID. They've played their game
In the dark: we're theirs, whoever calls us.

ADAMS. Stand at ease.

DAVID. Our feet are tied!

PETER. Hobbled,
Poor asses.

ADAMS. That leaves me without a word of command
Except fall on your knees.

PETER. What's coming, Corporal?

ADAMS. You two, let's know it: we have to meet the fire.

DAVID. Tied hand and foot: not men at all!

PETER. O how
Shall we think these moments out
Before thinking splits to fear. I begin

To feel the sweat of the pain: though the pain
Hasn't reached us yet.

ADAMS. Have your hearts ready:
It's coming now.

DAVID. Every damned forest in the world
Has fallen to make it. The glare's on us.

PETER. Dead on.
And here's the reconnoitring heat:
It tells us what shall come.

ADAMS. Now then! Chuck down
Your wishes for the world: there's nothing here
To charm us. Ready?

DAVID. I've been strong.
The smoke's between us. Where are you, Adams?

ADAMS. Lost.

PETER. Where are you, Adams?

[ADAMS *cries out and falls to his knees.*

DAVID. It's come to him, Peter!

PETER. We shall know!

DAVID. Scalding God!

[*They, too, have fallen to their knees.*

ADAMS. What way have I come down, to find
I live still, in this round of blaze?
Here on my knees. And a fire hotter
Than any fire has ever been
Plays over me. And I live. I know
I kneel.

DAVID. Adams.

ADAMS. We're not destroyed.

DAVID. Adams.

PETER. Voices. We're men who speak.

DAVID. We're men who sleep and wake.
They haven't let us go.

PETER. My breath
Parts the fire a little.

ADAMS. But the cords
That were tying us are burnt: drop off
Like snakes of soot.

PETER. Can we stand?

DAVID. Even against this coursing fire we can.

PETER. Stand: move: as though we were living,
In this narrow shaking street
Under the eaves of seven-storeyed flames
That lean and rear again, and still
We stand. Can we be living, or only
Seem to be?

ADAMS. I can think of life.
We'll make it yet.

DAVID. That's my devotion.
Which way now?

PETER. Wait a minute. Who's that
Watching us through the flame?

[MEADOWS, *a dream figure, is sitting on the side of his bunk.*

DAVID. Who's there?

ADAMS. Keep your heads down. Might be
Some sniper of the fire.

[MEADOWS *crows like a cock.*

PETER. A lunatic.

ADAMS [*calling to* MEADOWS]. Who are you?

MEADOWS. Man.

ADAMS. Under what command?

MEADOWS. God's.

ADAMS. May we come through?

MEADOWS. If you have
The patience and the love.

DAVID. Under this fire?

MEADOWS. Well, then, the honesty.

ADAMS. What honesty?

MEADOWS. Not to say we do
A thing for all men's sake when we do it only
For our own. And quick eyes to see
Where evil is. While any is our own
We sound fine words unsoundly.

ADAMS. You cockeyed son
Of heaven, how did you get here?

MEADOWS. Under the fence. I think they forgot
To throw me in. But there's not a skipping soul
On the loneliest goat-path who is not
Hugged into this, the human shambles.
And whatever happens on the farthest pitch,
To the sand-man in the desert or the island-man in the sea,
Concerns us very soon. So you'll forgive me
If I seem to intrude.

PETER. Do you mean to stay here?

MEADOWS. I can't get out alone. Neither can you.

But, on the other hand, single moments
Gather towards the striking clock.
Each man is the world.

PETER. But great events
Go faster.

DAVID. Who's to lead us out of this?

MEADOWS. It's hard to see. Who will trust
What the years have endlessly said?

ADAMS. There's been a mort of time. You'd think
Something might have come of it. These men
Are ready to go, and so am I.

PETER. But there's no God-known government anywhere.

MEADOWS. Behind us lie
The thousand and the thousand and the thousand years
Vexed and terrible. And still we use
The cures which never cure.

DAVID. For mortal sake,
Shall we move? Do we just wait and die?

MEADOWS. Figures of wisdom back in the old sorrows
Hold and wait for ever. We see, admire
But never suffer them: suffer instead
A stubborn aberration.
O God, the fabulous wings unused,
Folded in the heart.

DAVID. So help me, in
The stresses of this furnace I can see
To be strong beyond all action is the strength
To have. But how do men and forbearance meet?
A stone forbears when the wheel goes over, but that
Is death to the flesh.

ADAMS. And every standing day
The claims are deeper, inactivity harder.
But where, in the maze of right and wrong,
Are we to do what action?

PETER. Look, how intense
The place is now, with swaying and troubled figures.
The flames are men: all human. There's no fire!
Breath and blood chokes and burns us. This
Surely is unquenchable? It can only transform.
There's no way out. We can only stay and alter.

DAVID. Who says there's nothing here to hate?

MEADOWS. The deeds, not those who do.

ADAMS. Strange how we trust the powers that ruin
And not the powers that bless.

DAVID. But good's unguarded,
As defenceless as a naked man.

MEADOWS. Imperishably. Good has no fear;
Good is itself, what ever comes.
It grows, and makes, and bravely
Persuades, beyond all tilt of wrong:
Stronger than anger, wiser than strategy,
Enough to subdue cities and men
If we believe it with a long courage of truth.

DAVID. Corporal, the crowing son of heaven
Thinks we can make a morning.

MEADOWS. Not
By old measures. Expedience and self-preservation
Can rot as they will. Lord, where we fail as men
We fail as deeds of time.

PETER. The blaze of this fire
Is wider than any man's imagination.
It goes beyond any stretch of the heart.

MEADOWS. The human heart can go to the lengths of God.
Dark and cold we may be, but this
Is no winter now. The frozen misery
Of centuries breaks, cracks, begins to move;
The thunder is the thunder of the floes,
The thaw, the flood, the upstart Spring.
Thank God our time is now when wrong
Comes up to face us everywhere,
Never to leave us till we take
The longest stride of soul men ever took.
Affairs are now soul size.
The enterprise
Is exploration into God.
Where are you making for? It takes
So many thousand years to wake,
But will you wake for pity's sake?
Pete's sake, Dave or one of you,
Wake up, will you? Go and lie down.
Where do you think you're going?

ADAMS [*waking where he stands*]. What's wrong?

MEADOWS. You're walking in your sleep.
So's Pete and Dave. That's too damn many.

ADAMS. Where's this place? How did I get here?

MEADOWS. You were born here, chum. It's the same for all of us.
Get into bed.

PETER [*waking*]. What am I doing here?

MEADOWS. Walking your heart out, boy.

ADAMS. Dave, Dave.

MEADOWS. Let him come to himself gentle but soon
Before he goes and drowns himself in the font.

ADAMS. Wake up, Dave.

PETER. I wish I knew where I was.

MEADOWS. I can only give you a rough idea myself.
In a sort of a universe and a bit of a fix.
It's what they call flesh we're in.
And a fine old dance it is.

DAVID [*awake*]. Did they fetch us up?

MEADOWS. Out of a well. Where Truth was.
They didn't like us fraternizing. Corp,
Would you mind getting your men to bed
And stop them trapsing round the precincts?

ADAMS. Dave, we're mad boys. Sleep gone to our heads.
Come on.

DAVID. What's the time?

ADAMS. Zero hour.

DAVID. It feels like half an hour below. I've got cold feet.

PETER. [*already lying on his bunk*] I've never done that before. I wonder now
What gives us a sense of direction in a dream?
Can we see in sleep? And what would have happened
If we'd walked into the guard? Would he have shot us,
Thinking we were trying to get out?

MEADOWS. So you were from what you said. I could stand
One at a time, but not all three together.

It began to feel like the end of the world
With all your bunks giving up their dead.

ADAMS. Well, sleep, I suppose.

DAVID. Yeh. God bless.

PETER. Rest you merry.

MEADOWS. Hope so. Hope so.

[*They settle down. The church clock strikes. A bugle sounds in the distance.*

THE PLAY ENDS

THE DARK IS LIGHT ENOUGH

A Winter Comedy

To

LENA ASHWELL

with affection and admiration

CHRISTOPHER FRY EDITH EVANS

THE DARK IS LIGHT ENOUGH

First performed in London, at the Aldwych Theatre, on 30 April 1954

Jakob	JOHN MOFFAT
Kassel	PETER BULL
Belmann	HUGH GRIFFITH
Stefan	PETER BARKWORTH
Bella	VIOLET FAREBROTHER
Willi	DAVID SPENSER
Gelda	MARGARET JOHNSTON
Richard Gettner	JAMES DONALD
Countess Rosmarin Ostenburg	EDITH EVANS
Colonel Janik	JOHN GLEN
Count Peter Zichy	JACK GWILLIM
1st Soldier	PETER SALLIS
2nd Soldier	FREDERICK TREEVES
3rd Soldier	CHURTON FAIRMAN
1st Guard	PETER HALLIDAY
2nd Guard	GEORGE MURCELL

Produced by Peter Brook
Scenery and costumes by Oliver Messel

CHARACTERS

IN ORDER OF APPEARANCE

JAKOB
KASSEL
BELMANN
STEFAN
BELLA
WILLI
GELDA
RICHARD GETTNER
COUNTESS ROSMARIN OSTENBURG
COLONEL JANIK
COUNT PETER ZICHY
1ST SOLDIER
2ND SOLDIER
3RD SOLDIER
1ST GUARD
2ND GUARD

An Austrian country-house
near the Hungarian border

The winter of 1848–9

The weather was stormy; the sky heavily clouded; the darkness . . . profound. . . . It was across this maze of leafage, and in absolute darkness, that the butterflies had to find their way in order to attain the end of their pilgrimage.

Under such conditions the screech-owl would not dare to forsake its olive-tree. The butterfly . . . goes forward without hesitation. . . . So well it directs its tortuous flight that, in spite of all the obstacles to be evaded, it arrives in a state of perfect freshness, its great wings intact. . . . The darkness is light enough. . . .

J. H. FABRE

ACT ONE

A room and a great staircase

JAKOB. KASSEL.

Enter BELMANN.

JAKOB. Tell us, then, what in the world has happened?
Are we never to have any more Thursdays, Belmann?

BELMANN. The Countess is nowhere in the house.

KASSEL. I guessed as much
Before I was over the threshold. In fact
I had the thought of it half a mile away.
'I suppose this *is* Thursday', I said to myself,
And looked at my watch.

BELMANN. She drove away, alone,
Before light this morning.

JAKOB. Alone?

BELMANN. All the servants
Swear by heaven it's impossible, and by God
There's no doubt of it. One of them woke,
Or dreamt he woke, and heard, or thought he heard,
The great sleigh making for the Thiereck gate.
But now the snow's so deep there's no way of telling.

JAKOB. Not even towards Vienna? Towards Thiereck?
I wonder if she knows where the Hungarian troops are.
Surely she must have heard they're advancing?

KASSEL. With
A son-in-law in the War Ministry, she may well believe
They're where they were two months ago, still
Fighting the Serbs.

JAKOB. Do you think this is the time
To joke, Dr. Kassel? Think of the Countess.

KASSEL. I do, and the snow immediately melts
And all the Hungarians are dead.

JAKOB. But she left in absolute secret, before light,
Quite alone, and in this weather—

KASSEL. And on a Thursday,
That's the worst of it.

JAKOB. What are you mocking, Kassel?

KASSEL. I? Mocking? Dear fellow, my dear boy,
Nothing that doesn't mock me in return.

JAKOB. Isn't it true that in more than twenty years
She has only once before failed her Thursday,
When her son Stefan was born?

KASSEL. Not even once.
'Good God', she said, 'I think the monkey
Means to be born on Thursday evening.'
But she received us all at seven o'clock,
And at nine, when Gyorki was saying, as usual,
That there is no clear truth except the present
Which alters as we grasp it,
She bowed to us in the doorway, and said
'We must freely admit the future', and withdrew
To give birth to Stefan.

JAKOB. But what future
Can make her withdraw today and abandon her Thursday?

A message of two lines would have put our minds
At rest.

KASSEL. Do you think so? I have always found
Her handwriting to be her way, not
Of giving but of withholding information.
Don't we hear her now?

Enter STEFAN.

KASSEL. Well, Stefan, where's your mother?

STEFAN. That's just it,
Doctor Kassel, where's my mother?
The whole day I've been riding the country-side
Asking every person I could find.
One said he caught the sound of bells in the dark,
But the rest had never heard of a human being
Since they last went to mass. But she may tell you
Herself. Here's a letter for you.

KASSEL. Where did you find this?

STEFAN. Face-downwards. I've only this moment discovered it.

BELMANN. Now, Kassel. What has she to say? What is the answer
To the mystery?

KASSEL. She has taken some pains with this.
One guesses almost at once that words are meant.
Ah, yes. You see, now. In this world a mystery
Is only so out of extreme simplicity.

JAKOB. Read it, Kassel.

KASSEL. Yes, of course. She says:
'Dear my little doctor, if, and I don't
Know why it should be, when the evening comes
I am still not with you, do make my excuses.
Tell them not to talk about—', but here

The marks on the paper leave one a wide margin
Of possibility. Three words, apparently
Entirely composed of E's. 'Tell them not
To talk about Eel*ee*leeology,
Eel*ee*leeology, OR Eel*ee*leeology.
The world is more serious than that.
I have gone out. Your affectionate
Rosmarin Ostenburg.'

JAKOB. But I don't see, Kassel,
What we're supposed to make of it.

BELMANN. As Kassel says,
It's only too simple. The Countess, impatient
Of the doctor's attention, has gone out:
To pay a call, or to take a breath of air,
But for rather more than twelve hours, and in
The direction of a war.

STEFAN. But will you tell me
What I should have done, or do now, if my mother's lost?

BELMANN. Ah, there we have the difficulty.
This Thursday world of ours is now
More like the world than ever.
The goddess of it, in her Godlike way,
Is God knows where. We can only hope
She will condescend to appear in her own time.

JAKOB. No, no; we must be anxious. I should have
No peace for a moment if I thought I lacked anxiety.
You might pray for her safety, Belmann,
Instead of inventing crackpot blasphemies.

BELMANN. Blasphemies? Why do you think I blaspheme?
You know the Countess has the qualities of true divinity.
For instance: how apparently undemandingly

She moves among us; and yet
Lives make and unmake themselves in her neighbourhood
As nowhere else. There are many names I could name
Who would have been remarkably otherwise
Except for her divine non-interference.

KASSEL. Good heavens, she would rather be dead
Than be responsible for any change
In any soul in the world.

BELMANN. She can't escape it.
If she should die, her gravestone would play havoc
With the life of the mason who carved it.
She has a touching way
Of backing a man up against eternity
Until he hardly has the nerve to remain mortal.

STEFAN. My first thought, as it always is,
Was to tell my brother-in-law the trouble.
To me Peter treads the earth more surely
And reassures more instantly
Than any other man. So instinctively
In the morning panic, I sent a message
To Peter and my sister in Vienna.

KASSEL. Have you had an answer?

STEFAN. Nothing yet.
But Peter's the great protector of the family.
If you call to him, he puts his own world down
And takes yours up, almost before you realize
What made you need him.
But I thought none of you would be here tonight.
We're in the direct road of the revolution.
The peasants are saying their dogs haven't stopped barking
Since before sunset. They hear the shake

Of marching in the earth. It's a wretched business.
The Hungarians have managed to exist
Happily enough in the Empire up to now.
And Peter is Hungarian, after all,
And still finds it possible to serve
In the Austrian Government.
But these Hungarian nationalists think they stand
For truth and light, and kill accordingly.
It would have been wiser to have stayed in Vienna.

BELMANN. My commitment, on Thursday evenings, is to be here.
After that I will be wise or not as I may be.
A man has to provide his own providence
Or there's no knowing what religion will get hold of him.

STEFAN. Why aren't you drinking? Make Bella bring you something. [*He goes upstairs.*

KASSEL. Yes, yes; we won't let ourselves be forgotten.

BELMANN. All the servants are in their accustomed places;
Only the virtue has gone out of them.

[*He pulls a bell-rope.*

What, Kassel, you say the Countess would never
Change a soul? And yet you and I can remember
How ten years ago this great and good
Lady of our imagination
Conscripted her little daughter, Gelda,
Then aged—what was she, Kassel?—sixteen at most—

KASSEL. Seventeen.

BELMANN. —then aged seventeen,
Into a marriage with that rag of hell
Richard Gettner: that invertebrate,
That self-drunk, drunken, shiftless, heartless,
Lying malingerer, Richard Gettner,

Than whom of all the tribe of men
There was no man more likely to make her wretched.

JAKOB. Liar, Belmann, a wicked lie!

BELMANN. Did you ever
Know Richard Gettner?

JAKOB. No, at school I read
His first book, whatever the name of it was,
When everyone said it would give literature
A new fire. I never met him,
Or read another.

BELMANN. There wasn't another.
He fled from his one book as though his own
Reality had struck him on the mouth.
And then, on the profits from it, became a pest
Who never left us, and never loved us;
Unreliable when he was drunk,
Irresponsible when he was sober,
Useless to any world, sober or drunk.
But the Countess thought she should marry her daughter to him,
I imagine to celebrate the tenth reprinting.

JAKOB. The Countess can be sure, wherever she may be,
Her name is safe in this house, even though
It means the end of one of us, either you or me.
Discuss this with pistols, as soon as you like:
Tomorrow or Saturday.

BELMANN. Don't be troublesome,
Jakob.

KASSEL. Preposterous. Ring the bell again.

JAKOB. No, no, I mean it. At last I can show myself
What these evenings have meant to me. I shall fight you.

BELMANN. We shall miss you, Jakob.
Let us, by all means, shoot at one another
If you think it will improve human nature.
And what is to happen after that?

JAKOB. I'm only
Concerned with this moment of loyalty.

BELMANN. I respect it:
But don't question my integrity.

JAKOB. Very well; I call you a liar.

BELMANN. Well, so I sometimes am.
But don't question my integrity.
It was an act of dark night
To marry her daughter to him. And, thank God,
He was mad, or no man, or had some faint
Kick of conscience, enough to make him have mercy
And never touch her. And so for a time
She walked in his house looking in the mirrors
And after a few months came away,
And the Church dissolved all, as though
Mortal mistakes were snow; and she was married
To Count Peter the sturdy. By so small
A margin was misery missed and her mother undamned.

Enter BELLA, *and* WILLI, *a servant*, *with refreshment.*

KASSEL. Bella, we need you. We're thirsty, anxious,
And unattended. Why wouldn't you come to us?

BELLA. Dr. Kassel, you mustn't say so. If I could always do what's impossible I should have very great advantages. But when you rang the bell, she was there, with every bell on the harness ringing, arriving at the old entrance.

KASSEL. Who arriving, Bella?

JAKOB. Do you mean the Countess? Is she home again, Bella?

BELLA. Then where is Willi, or Spier, you may say, or old Tenky? But don't think, because she can take herself off in the morning without help from a soul, she doesn't come back in the evening, looking as helpless as though no coat would come off without two able-bodied men to each sleeve.

BELMANN. In fact, the Countess is with us again.

KASSEL. Well, Bella, where has she been?

BELLA. She says she isn't at all certain because everywhere is so alike in the snow. She says she prayed to be punctual, but, considering the time of year, she didn't pray nearly enough. I'm just going up to her.

KASSEL. Tell her, if she's tired—and how the devil can she not be?—not to dream of coming down to us. It's a great foolishness. Tell her, if you like, I forbid it.

BELLA. You know very well, Dr. Kassel, she would come down before she was ready, in case you thought there was any doubt of it.

BELMANN. So after all, Willi, your mistress has come back, and it seems there's no trouble.

WILLI. That's it, sir. The gentleman has the trouble, dear God he has, I should say so, speaking in regard to him, sir.

BELMANN. Gentleman, Willi? What gentleman?

BELLA. Don't encourage him, sir. He sees gentlemen everywhere. Every day I have to tell him there's no such thing. Is there such a thing, Willi? Now think with your head.

WILLI. No, mam.

BELLA. So go downstairs, Willi.

WILLI. Yes, mam.

[*He goes.*

BELLA. It's best to say nothing, and the gentlemen pass off. We're none of us perfect. There's her bell again.

[*She goes away up the stairs.*

BELMANN. So saying, the world was emptied of men.

JAKOB. It would be all the better for it, if many men
Were as unmannered as you are.
To insinuate so, in front of a servant:
'What gentleman, Willi?' Are you trying deliberately
To infuriate me?

BELMANN. Truth, Jakob,
Truth, is what my knees bow to.
Kassel, something approximating
To a suspicion of the truth has just occurred to me.
What more likely than that Richard Gettner's
Behind this mystery?

KASSEL. Gettner?

BELMANN. Where is the onetime bridegroom now?

JAKOB. With the Hungarian army, I know, I heard that.

BELMANN. With the Hungarian army: off he went
Roaring into their arms, the great lover
Of his country's enemies. Indeed, loving
The enemy is almost the only commandment
He's never broken. Whoever hates his race,
His Emperor, his culture, or his mother
Wins—well, not his heart, which is apparently
Only locomotor,
But all the enthusiasm of his spleen.

BELLA *comes down the stairs with* STEFAN.

BELLA. Oh, goodness now, somebody's come, and I think it's

your sister, but what in the world, what a thing to do, if it is your sister, what a thing to have happened in the circumstances.

STEFAN. Yes, Bella, what a thing to have happened. Is Count Peter with her?

BELLA. How can I tell? The window's caked with snow, and you breathe whatever you do. Well, I'll have a little word with her first and give her fair warning, and that's the best I can do, and there we are.

[*She hurries out.*

STEFAN [*to* KASSEL]. What mystery is there now?

KASSEL. Mystery, my dear boy? Because Bella is mysterious?
What nonsense.

A MAN *is slowly descending the stairs.*

BELMANN. No, but a little mystery there may be.
Willi has seen visions of gentlemen
Or at least one gentleman, to our perfect knowledge—

JAKOB. Belmann, I wish I could strike you dead!

BELMANN. On Saturday, Jakob. Don't fuss.

STEFAN. Why, what goes on?
What gentleman?

Enter GELDA, *followed by* BELLA.

GELDA. Stefan, what happened? Where
Did mother go?

BELLA. If only you weren't so impatient
And had let me speak to you.

STEFAN. Oh, Gelda, I'm sorry:
This was my bad blunder. Has Peter come?

[GELDA *is looking at the* MAN, *who has reached the foot of the stairs.*

KASSEL [*turning*]. Richard Gettner!

BELLA. There it is, you see.

[*She goes out.*

JAKOB. Gettner?

BELMANN. Gettner, by God!

GETTNER. By God, no other.
I remember you, too, but without astonishment.
It's Thursday night. The intellectual soul
Of Europe comes down to the stream to drink. What's this
Floating belly-upwards? A dead fish?
Gettner, by God!

KASSEL. Now, come: why not allow us
A perfectly natural surprise?

BELMANN. We thought
You played games in a different alley now.

GETTNER. I'm surprised that you should have me in your thoughts.

GELDA. Richard, make me some sign of recognition.

GETTNER. Why? You must know I recognize you.
But then you also know, I suppose, the ten
Years have improved you to a kind of beauty,
And you'd like to see that I see that.
Well, if it gives you pleasure to be commended
By what remains of a bad husband,
Be pleased: I've noticed and admired.
Where's your *good* husband this vile night?

BELMANN. That's charming, Gettner.

GELDA. Peter will be here presently.
He said he would follow after, the first moment
He could manage to get away. We were both
Anxious for my mother.

GETTNER. Said he would follow
After? God in heaven, is this the night
For members of His Imperial Majesty's Government
To send their young wives on country visits?
And themselves to follow after? Is he a fool,
Your good husband? I know the snow tonight
Comes down as white and soft as a bishop's hand
But the blessing falls on a night on earth
When any man's death is right for someone or other.
Is he a fool, your husband?

GELDA. Where was my mother
All through today?

GETTNER. The roads are very sour
With men marching. He should know that, dear God.

GELDA. Where was my mother?

BELMANN. And where were you, Gettner?
Tell me, who called the Countess out
On to the very roads you mention. Who
Was the fool who did it?
And how do you come to be here? Are you
Dining with enemies tonight?

GELDA. Now
There are no questions I want to ask you, Richard.
You should know there are friends here, as there always have been.

KASSEL. Quite so, Belmann, we don't want this catechism.
We can be inquisitive by degrees.

BELMANN. I don't agree, Kassel. A man can't know
How to conduct himself towards another man
Without the answer to certain basic questions.
What does the man choose to believe? What good

And evil has he invented for himself?
In short, how has he made himself exist?
And then, the crux of it all,
Does his chosen existence agree
With the good and evil I invent for myself?
Only then—

KASSEL. You're being pompous, Belmann.

BELMANN. I choose to be pompous. And will Gettner please
Choose to make his existence plain?

GETTNER. I think
It's plainer in your words, Belmann, than ever
It would be in mine.

BELMANN. Will you admit you joined
The Hungarian army?

GETTNER. Certainly.
It was on a Sunday, between five and six.

BELMANN. Indeed? Then what business have you here?

GETTNER. I was born a casual, unacceptable visitor.

BELMANN. Into what world, it seems, you've never discovered.

KASSEL. Then for heaven's sake be quiet and let him wonder.

BELMANN. We have to make sense of this. We know that arms
Are moving through the night against Vienna.
But here's a stray of the enemy's
Who seems to think he can wander anywhere.

GETTNER. I should never grudge a man
Such a pretty moment of conversion
As I had that Sunday. A wet and windy Sunday.
All the streets were in a holy stupor
Except for the mad bashing of the cathedral bells.
Bash, crash, take that for your damned impudent

Soul, they said: in the name of the Father, the Son,
And the Holy Ghost, bash, bash: we'll lay you
Flat in the mud of Crown Prince Rudolf Street,
You dust. And all I could do for my self-esteem
Was to swear to cherish all hearts that are oppressed;
To give myself to liberty, justice, and the revolution.

STEFAN. And the lynching of Count Latour on Buda bridge.

GETTNER. There are fearful excitements on any side.
Any side can accuse the other
And feel virtuous without the hardships of virtue.
When pride of race has been pent up
In a tyrannous disregard, and valued liberties
Have been lost for long enough, what comes in the way
Of dignity's free and natural flowing
Is nothing but rocks to be blasted. I envy them
Their certainty. Each private man
Has a public cause to elucidate him,
And a reasonable sense of having been wronged.
If you like you can call this man your enemy;
It's what he expects.

BELMANN. And now, if you like,
Will you tell us how the war goes on without you,
And what interesting manœuvre you've been carrying out today?

Enter the COUNTESS.

COUNTESS. You will not make an interruption of me,
But think I was here from the beginning of the evening;
So I shall know you forgive me.

GELDA. Mother—

JAKOB. Dear Countess—

KASSEL. I don't know that I shall
Forgive you, Rosmarin.

COUNTESS. Of course you will.
But if all the crooked places of the world
Have been made plain to you while I was out,
That I shall not forgive.

BELMANN. I assure you, more crooked than ever.

COUNTESS. How few you are. Can so many
Of my friends have died in a week? I was anxious
You should all be astonished to hear
That this morning, by the confusing light
Of one lantern I harnessed the horses, poor angels,
With my own insufficient hands. Will you believe me?

STEFAN. We've already marvelled.

GELDA. But why did you treat us
As though we cared nothing about you at all?

COUNTESS. Chaffinch, I have to be very vexed with you.
You should not be here; you should be safe in Vienna.

GELDA. But we thought you were lost and dead.

COUNTESS. Yet when
Have I ever done anything to make you think so?

STEFAN. Why, today you did.

COUNTESS. Indeed
I am contrite, and very humble, and enchanted
By the perils of the day, because today
I have been as clever as an ostler,
And driven alone, one human and two horses,
Into a redeemed land, uncrossed by any soul
Or sound, and always the falling perfection
Covering where we came, so that the land
Lay perfect behind us, as though we were perpetually
Forgiven the journey. And moreover
A strange prescience possessed me.

One must have talent to go from a place to a place,
But divination to go so deviously
That north, south, east, and west
Are lost in admiration, and *yet* to arrive,
After a short experience of eternity,
At the place and people one set out to reach:
Namely, to find, in a little farm
Fallen right out of the world in a drift of snow,
Poor hunted Richard.

BELMANN. Hunted?

GELDA. Why do you say
Poor hunted Richard?

COUNTESS. Poor Richard, he is hunted.

KASSEL. Now, Rosmarin, throw some light on this.
No more mystery.

COUNTESS. Physician dear,
What mystery? Nothing in the world has been hidden,
Only Richard, who has lain for three nights in a barn.

GETTNER. I'm a deserter, simply, I expect
You understand that.

STEFAN. A deserter, simply!

KASSEL. Good God!

COUNTESS. Why are you shocked?
He has left them with a whole army but one.
Can they not be perfectly troublesome with that?

BELMANN. In my stupidity I seem to be
One conversion behind. To what dear cause
Are you devoted tonight? What hearts
Do you cherish at present?

GETTNER. None.
The Hungarians, I see and admire it,
Have a cause, and a passion vigorous enough
To be called a virtue.
But rights exist: causes, faiths, truths,
High thoughts and righteous judgements
Which aren't for me. Boredom and melancholy
Drove me nearly mad.
There's a dreariness in dedicated spirits
That makes the promised land seem older than the fish.

BELMANN. Let me regard him after I've drunk a little.
My glass is empty.

KASSEL. Rosmarin, one thing interests me, when
You set out this morning, how far did you foresee
The danger of your ways? Or, if I may say so,
How well do you realize it even now?

COUNTESS. Little doctor, what do you say to me?
I know the true world, and you know I do.
But we needn't let it think we all bow down.
I haven't forgotten it. Indeed, today
As we turned the horses' heads
I heard the true world singing on the march;
The Hungarian army on the other side of the hill
Sounded like a pack of dogs in cry
To Richard's ears and mine.

STEFAN. I don't know how you tolerate him.
He's a man half-way through his life
With no infirmity except himself,
And yet you let him drag you out
To endure the toughest day, merely
To rescue him from his own feeble fault.

COUNTESS. Nonsense, Stefan. It was all a very simple matter,
Only complicated by the weather.

GELDA. We know too little to make a judgement yet.
We should only care
Richard is out of this unhappy war.
Here there's no war, Stefan.

KASSEL. No; but still
There may be presently. Surely our concern
Is not whether Gettner should be held responsible
For the snowfall, or whether or not
He should have considered the danger and the distance—
Indeed, he may not have taken into account
That your mother would circle half round the kingdom—

GETTNER. Doctor,
Don't let's give me any imaginary virtues.
I'd have prayed and begged and bullied her to fetch me
If the roads had been under fire and water,
If the distance and the danger had been trebled
And death not unlikely.
There was no one else I could believe would come;
Except the firing-squad, which I was not
In the mood to welcome.

BELMANN. I could do its work
With my own trigger-finger, without a qualm.

GELDA. He sent for help to this house.
But what help can there ever be for Richard?

KASSEL. Our present concern is whether the Hungarians
Mean to let you disappear so easily.
Your name has the ring of reputation,
And I suppose you may have information

Which they might think valuable to their success.
And that being so—

GETTNER. I am infectious, doctor.
You're quite right. I carry the war with me:
None of you can be altogether
Unconcerned, if the Hungarians come
This way, till the army passes with its singing
On to the Vienna road. Until
The snow falls back again to its quiet heaping
Over this house, I'm bound to give you
Great uneasiness. This disease I am
You're all of you guilty of harbouring
Against the liberalities in arms
Who mean to shoot me like a dog. I am sorry
If you should have to take this war seriously.

JAKOB. It's true what he says; Countess, did you think of it?
Suppose they come this way, and suppose by some chance
They know where Gettner's hiding, may it not
Be very unpleasant, most of all for you
Who in your innocence of heart brought him among us?

COUNTESS. Innocent?
I am always perfectly guilty of what I do,
Thank God.

BELMANN. Countess, you see we're here in a trap
With you and this gentleman of uncertain future.
May we presume to doubt your wisdom and care for us?

JAKOB. No, I never wish to doubt you, Countess,
Nor to hear you doubted! Whatever I reverence
Can be sure of me, as there's a man shall know
On Friday.

BELMANN. Saturday, I thought.

KASSEL. Now, now, come along.

COUNTESS. It's very hard to follow you. Saturday you thought,
Or Friday. But I've been lost already
So many times today, it begins to seem
No great misfortune. Let us say
We are all confused, incomprehensible,
Dangerous, contemptible, corrupt,
And in that condition pass the evening
Thankfully and well. In our plain defects
We already know the brotherhood of man.
Who said that?

BELMANN. You, Countess.

COUNTESS. How interesting.
I thought it was a quotation.

GELDA. But the night
Is still a danger for Richard.

JAKOB. For us, too.

STEFAN. And for Peter, which is worse.
We should send Gettner out into the night again
And let it beat on his own head alone.

GELDA. You don't know what you're saying, Stefan.

STEFAN. I know whose life I value.

GETTNER. For how much longer, I wonder, am I to be
Kept standing in the pillory,
Diagnosed unsatisfactory
By these gentlemen of high soul.
I was never to their liking, nor they to mine
That I can remember,
But perhaps they will agree to let me live
Though it may be some trouble to them. This

I do know, I'll not die to oblige anybody;
Nor for the sake of keeping up
Decent appearances. Before I do
I'll get down on all fours, foot-kissing,
Dust-licking, belly-crawling,
And any worm can have me for an equal,
Rather than I should have no life at all.

BELMANN. Well, that, I think, is clear.
You have a remarkably short distance to go.

GELDA. Oh, Richard, why do you have to destroy every
Way of coming to you?

GETTNER. Let me be honest.
I suppose I'm very little else.

GELDA. I don't know why I should seem
To owe shame to you all for Richard. He is, after all,
His own man, no less if he feels like a child,
And, I know, no care of mine.

STEFAN. Of course he's no care of yours.
Why should he cling round this family, and put
You to shame and mother into danger?

COUNTESS. So shamefully,
I seem to have gone floating out
Of this interesting present
To some remote evening, a no-man's country.
Now it seems to me very strange
You should all be so occupied in living.

KASSEL. You're not well; you have driven yourself too hard
For too long, Rosmarin.

GELDA. Darling, you need rest.
Leave us now and get some sleep.

JAKOB. Dear Countess—

COUNTESS. No, no, no. It's the perfection of sleep
To be awake to the dream.
If I were going to live for ever
This would be the way: unconcerned
And yet reasonably fond. I am like an arm or a hand
After a rigorous long time unflexing.
It unclenches at last into an apparition
And touches without feeling
It is so disenchanted of the body.
I am altogether so, now that the day is over.
And I look far back to us all where we are living
Uncertain people in an uncertain time,
And it seems long ago. But I confuse you.
To you the time is close
And sharp and prevailing. And I shall pray,
If prayers can make me serious, that tomorrow
I may concentrate on my responsibilities.
Till then, for my sake, if my sake is worthy,
Be like men waiting.

GETTNER. Listen, do you hear that?

KASSEL. Hear what?

JAKOB. Countess, you heard
The Hungarian army singing, did you not?

GELDA. Was it like any sound you hear at the moment?
Listen.

KASSEL. Ah! Then I caught something.

COUNTESS. I am not sure you should listen. If it's the same
Song that came to us over the hill
Richard told me it was not proper. But that

Was several hours ago, although of course
If it's very improper perhaps they never get tired of it.

GETTNER. Where are they now?

JAKOB. Not far.

STEFAN. But listen: where's the singing? Surely
It's died away.

JAKOB. But it didn't pass us by.

COUNTESS. Why should it? No one sings for ever.
Let them take breath.

[JAKOB *throws open the window. Military orders are being shouted some distance away.*

STEFAN. Do you hear that?

GETTNER. They haven't passed the gates.
What Godforgotten bastard saw us
Turn in here, and told them? Now it comes.

COUNTESS. Jakob, do shut the window.
It's very cold. You will give us all pneumonia.

GETTNER. Where shall I go? If they're coming to search the house
Where are you going to hide me? Will you remember
This hour is life and death for me?

GELDA. Do you think
We haven't understood that?

COUNTESS. It is disappointing.
I had begun to be eternally dispassionate,
And life and death at once become the argument.
But don't distrust me, Richard.
I hope I shall do better
Than throw away the gains of the day
To the first indignant animal who comes.

You can, if you like, climb to the little bell-turret
And draw the rope ladder up after you.
The dirt and spiders and discomfort there
In a filthy way will give the illusion of safety.
But there is still time for nothing to happen.
After all, an army must sometimes halt,
And why not here? Their heels are lumped with snow
And they can kick them clean against my gates
And so march on as light as boys
For a yard or two. Though when I think tonight
May be the last of human time
For some of them, I wish their feet
So very heavy and slow
They could live long lives on the road.

[*A hammering on the outside door. Enter* BELLA.

BELLA. Madam,
The worst of it is, the house is surrounded by soldiers.
What am I to do about the knocking, madam?

COUNTESS. If you wish the door
Still to be there to open tomorrow, open it, Bella.

BELLA. Shall I let them in with their guns? If they should ask?

COUNTESS. I believe we can't expect to separate them.

BELLA. They can click their heels at me as much as they like,
They won't make me think it's natural manners.

[*Exit* BELLA.

GETTNER. Who can I trust here? I know I offend
These gentlemen's opinion of the world,
And not one of them cares what becomes of me.

KASSEL. Gettner, Gettner, have some respect for yourself.

GETTNER. Have a respect for my life,

For the sake of your sleep to come, don't betray me.
Go to your imaginations, gentlemen:
Think of death by shooting.

BELMANN. I should more likely weep for stags or partridges.

COUNTESS. Do, then. Weep for what you can.
It's grateful to our brevity
To weep for what is briefer,
For nothing else will.

GETTNER [*leaning from the landing of the stairs*].
Lie, lie! O Christ, lie for me!

Re-enter BELLA.

BELLA [*closing the door behind her*].
Well, madam, he's a gentleman at least,
And I'm glad to say we know him: Colonel Janik,
Madam, but very peremptory.

COUNTESS. The geologist!
I remember him; ask him to come in.

BELLA. And what is so strange, I thought I saw
In the dark behind him—

COUNTESS. But I still think
We'd better not keep him waiting.

BELLA. Of course it was dark
And there seemed a great many faces, and all with their eyes
Looking straight at me, but there among all those Hungarians—

COUNTESS. Well, Bella, if you will not open the door
I must do it myself.

COLONEL JANIK *comes in without being admitted.*

JANIK. You will excuse me, Countess.
When there is peace I have more patient manners.

COUNTESS. I remember you with great pleasure, Colonel Janik.

JANIK. Other days, madam, are other days;
I must ask you not to remind me of them.

COUNTESS. I see
You have something urgent to say to me, Colonel,
And I will not waste your time by asking
Who you know here. I am with my friends and children.

JANIK. I would keep you so, Countess, and all other
Women too. We've been taking a buffeting
Out on the roads. You were sensible
To stay indoors today.

COUNTESS. You give me credit
For more sense than I can truthfully claim, Colonel.

JANIK. Indeed? It was very courageous of you, Countess
Whatever business forced you out, no doubt
Was harsh and necessary. Any postponement
Was impossible?

COUNTESS. Colonel, the time is passing.
Perhaps you too have business harsh and necessary.
You mustn't let me be the cause of delay.
We should deny ourselves the pleasure of strategy,
Though I very much admire
How cleverly you invest my position
Under cover of peaceful manœuvre.
But now I think we should have the charge direct.

JANIK. What does the name Captain Gettner
Mean to you, Countess?

COUNTESS. A fantasy, Colonel.

JANIK. I trusted you to be serious, but I see,
Madam, you mean to play.

COUNTESS. I was astonished
For a moment, you must let me be astonished,
Though I should know the world has many surprises
And Richard with a commission might possibly
Be one of them.

JANIK. I wish I might convey
The pressure of tonight and dawn tomorrow
Which is on my heart,
And ask you, therefore, to respect it.

COUNTESS. Colonel
You can be certain I do; but you mustn't expect
All men to leave their gentler world for yours.

JANIK. It has been reported that you were seen
With Captain Gettner in your sleigh;
That you apparently brought him to this house.

COUNTESS. It is a house to which I bring my friends.

JANIK. You may not have understood that Captain Gettner
Is a deserter.

COUNTESS. What else could he possibly be?
Suppose our friend has found himself
No longer bound in understanding to you,
Either in the pursuit of meaning or in any
Wholehearted belief, what except a deserter
Can he possibly be? He might not have supposed
You would let him resign and send him off
With your blessing on his way.

JANIK. This is a night
For simplicities, madam. I have two thousand men
Standing in the snow, their lives my trust.
Peace may go in search of the one soul
But we are not at peace.

COUNTESS. *You* are not
At peace, Colonel.

JANIK. Captain Gettner
Has broken his oath to the Hungarian Diet.
Captain Gettner has deserted in the field.
Captain Gettner, by the information
He possesses, has become too threatening
To my cause and country. For your one man
I have many, Countess, and I'm here
To arrest him. If you wish to abide
By your neutrality, madam, bring him out.
Otherwise, I regret, we shall come in and find him.

COUNTESS. I have no weapons to prevent you, Colonel.
The house will go down before you like matchwood.
Your victory will be complete, if not glorious.
Though I wonder you should think
So unhopefully of your own argument
That you meekly and unmanfully give in
To violence, when I am ready
To be persuaded to your opinion
By any truth which in God's world
You can put before me. I realize readily
Time is your anxiety, but in the end
Who drives the right way drives the fastest,
As only today I have been reminded.
I give you one promise: I shall never make
Myself, or my friends, my way of life
Or private contentment, or any
Preference of my nature, an obstacle
To the needs of a more true and living world
Than so far I have understood. Only
Tell me what is in this war you fight

Worth all your dead and suffering men.
Your faith is, your country has been refused
Its good rights, for many years too long.
So be certain, whatever the temptation,
No man is made a slave by you.
To you Austria is a tyranny.
Then, to the number of those men who die,
And far beyond that number infinitely,
Surely you will show
One man over another has no kingdom.
Otherwise, how shall I understand your war?
Because I have respect for Richard Gettner's
Wandering and uncertain will, *therefore*
I have respect for your sheer purpose
And for those many men I cannot
Know by name who are waiting in the snow.
But if you tell me Richard Gettner
Has thrown away his claim to freedom
By claiming that a man is free, then you
And those in the snow, may as well march
Against your guns and swords. They are tyrannous, too.
Is it not a quaint freedom, that lets us
Make up our minds and not be free to change them?
Poor hope for me! I change my mind
For pure relaxation, two or three times a day,
As I get wiser or sillier, whichever it is I do.
Must I save your cause for you, Colonel?
If so, then not in my name or Richard Gettner's
But in the name of all your nameless fellows
Who trust their suffering is righteous
I forbid you to invade the liberties of this house.

JANIK. For your sake, madam, I would love
Anarchy if I could. To search this house

And your estate will be a dangerous delay for us.
Instead, I offer you a free choice.
I have someone with me under my charge
Who may help us to a peaceful understanding.

[*He opens the door.*

Corporal, give Count Zichy my compliments
And ask him to be kind enough to let us have his company.

STEFAN. Peter! Now what damage have I done?

GELDA. What do they do with Peter?

BELMANN. Is this quite in good warfare, Colonel,
To have taken prisoner a civilian
Of such distinction, going about his peaceful
Business?

JANIK. If I were you, sir, I should not
Draw my attention to you.

Enter COUNT PETER.

GELDA. Peter blessed,
What has happened?

PETER. They were at the gate to welcome me.

JANIK. Count Zichy, we need you to show us the way to agree.

PETER. In this house we have always agreed fairly enough, Colonel.
You have your field of war; you should keep to it.

COUNTESS. But I have enlarged it to include myself,
Peter, so the Colonel tells me. Alas,
Peter, I am hotly debatable ground.

STEFAN. Peter, I brought this on you.

PETER. No such thing;
Time and place have conspired against us.

JANIK. That is one conspiracy for another,
And of the two it seems the fairer. So,
Countess, time and place give you a choice;
If you give up Gettner to answer for himself,
We free Count Zichy, and no further action
Is taken against this house.
Or the Count remains our prisoner and marches with us.
By bringing Gettner to this house, to meet the Count
And pass his information to the government,
You have done worse by us, I hope
Your goodness tells you, than we are doing to you.

STEFAN. Wrong!

COUNTESS. You are wrong.

GELDA. No such thing could happen.

STEFAN. Wrong, wrong, Colonel! It was all
A ridiculous chance. I sent for the Count
Only because I was afraid for my mother.

JANIK. That
May be, I don't know, but we're not without the danger.
Choose, Countess. My men are in the cold.
It is time you gave us Gettner, and let us go.

COUNTESS. Colonel, no man is mine to give you.

PETER. Bargaining with family affection, Colonel,
Isn't war. As I know this house, you have my word
There's been no conspiracy.

JANIK. So on your word
My men can pride themselves, as they go into battle,
That I failed to lead them even to the arrest
Of one deserter from the hands of a woman
Because of the word of the Emperor's Government.

Sir, for many centuries we have been able
To judge the word of the Emperor's Government.

PETER. You should know I love Hungary.

JANIK. I know that you're Hungarian. I know
Your voice in the Austrian Council must of course
Be moderate. I do not know
You love Hungary.

PETER. How shall I tell you
I love Hungary? Your love goes to war,
Mine stays at home, and there's no comparison:
You march with Buda-Pesth, and I reason with Vienna.
You have the benefit of passion, Colonel:
The world can see you with your life held high
Ready to hurl it out of your living hand
For the sake of Hungary, even perhaps
To lose the life of Hungary, too; and Hungary loves you.
Whereas, whatever I wish, in fact I see
Hungary's best future in Austria's friendship,
And I remain, if you like, the fool
Of my own faith and fallibility,
And Hungary scorns me; there's no comparison.
I see you love Hungary, I think it may be
To Hungary's sorrow. For me, there's nothing to show;
But indeed there can be love without evidence.

JANIK. Yes, yes; you're perfectly sincere,
You will always do what you can;
We're not ungrateful for your interest.
Count Zichy; it's only a pity
There's no better world fit to receive it.
But, excuse me, I think even in your world of paper
Desertion in the field has consequences.
Isn't it so?

PETER. It is so.

JANIK. Choose, Countess.

COUNTESS. There is no choice.

STEFAN No, there's no choice. By our fault
And his good nature, Peter's a prisoner.
And we're prisoners in Peter until he's free.
There's no question of choosing.

JANIK. Well, then, Countess.

COUNTESS. You put me very near the hard heart of the world,
Colonel, where bad and good eat at the same table.
No man is mine to give you.

STEFAN. Will you give him
Peter, then? Eyes of God,
Will you give him Peter?

COUNTESS. I may never know
What it is I do in the eyes of God.

STEFAN. Will someone less than God, and more than me,
Tell my mother what she is doing? Doctor
Kassel, will you tell her?

PETER. Stefan,
As less than God and more than you, I tell you
To hold your tongue. Deep water is for those
Who can swim.

STEFAN. I see.

KASSEL. Still, if I thought you wanted another opinion,
Rosmarin, I should give my opinion against you.

BELMANN. Philosophically, Countess, you may be reasonable,
But humanly I see no point of balance
Between a man and a rat.

JAKOB. There's no
Faith in Gettner, that's evident: I see
No doubt of which of the two is worthy.
I can't believe in a spiritual democracy.

BELMANN. Countess, when Jakob and I agree
It is time to consider.

COUNTESS. I have your own words, Peter,
For my comfort; there can be love without evidence.
No one can know how unwillingly I fail you,
But if it could be known, you of all men
Should know it. I believe
And witness you love Hungary, though in these times
You make yourself separate as an enemy.
Will you believe of me
That I decide against my love
With as much distress?

PETER. I hope I do:
I know I do, with what humility I have,
And I wish there were no conceit in me
To let me bid myself against another man.

JANIK. You must excuse me, Count Zichy, but I have
To ask you to leave with me. It isn't the way
I should wish to bring you among your countrymen,
But you come among them, and even that
I incline to welcome. Come, now.

STEFAN. Gelda—you fetch Gettner here!
You're the only one of us now
Who may persuade him.

JAKOB. That's true, certainly.
Not even Gettner would harden his heart against you.

BELMANN. Well, we shall see. For myself, I have
A less heroic opinion of him.

STEFAN. So, Gelda,
Go to him, find him, plead with him.
Colonel, I assure you—my sister will bring Gettner.

GELDA. Make my mother go, who brought him here.

STEFAN. You know my mother has refused. You have
The best right to go. Peter's your husband.

GELDA. Richard was my husband.

STEFAN. Gelda! What are you saying?

GELDA. You know Richard was my husband; though
It was only in a word, but still a word
Stays in the mind and has its children too.
I am Peter's wife, and everything
Is so well with us, our marriage vows
Go on like dancers, with no thought in the world to carry.
Only to be as easy and loving as we are.
But I was Richard's wife, and those vows,
Though they're cancelled and nowhere now,
Were abounding in purpose then, looking ahead
With eyes narrowed against the weather
To make a way where there was no way.
By which anxious journey we might have progressed
Beyond our selves to ourselves made wiser.
But we wouldn't venture.
Peter, if you rest in our love as I do,
Don't wish me to ask Richard to die.

PETER. There's no fear of that; no one need ever die
For us; you know I understand.
My God, I should be sorry to see
A dead man cross our love. Why, it's as much

For us as for him that you refuse to persuade him.
So say good-bye, with clear hearts, both of us.
In the order of things, when events will have it,
I shall come stolidly home.
We shall think nothing of this presently.

JANIK. Count Zichy.

PETER. Coming.

COUNTESS. Colonel Geologist,
You would do better to love your rocks and ammonites
Than flog your heart with your fellow countrymen.
You have such a dangerous, partial love.
Guard you, Peter.

PETER. Guard you, Rosmarin.

GELDA. What am I doing, Peter?

PETER. There's nothing
You need to wonder. All goes well.

[*He goes through the door.* JANIK *salutes and follows him.*
A pause.

STEFAN. He didn't look at me. He knows
I brought this on him.

BELMANN. If ever there was a bad exchange we've seen it now.
I feel indignant and aggrieved.

KASSEL. And I seriously wonder
Whether the drive you took so far in the snow,
Rosmarin, is finished even yet.

BELMANN. No good can come of it.

JAKOB. No good will ever come of Gettner.

COUNTESS. That may be true.

[STEFAN *opens the window. They hear the shouting of military commands as the* COUNTESS *goes up the stairs.*

THE CURTAIN FALLS

ACT TWO

The stables

GETTNER *is standing on a manger looking through a small, high, round window. The sound of a door opening and shutting.* GETTNER *jumps off the manger and runs across to a ladder leading up to a loft. In each side-pocket he carries a bottle. Enter* STEFAN.

STEFAN. You don't have to run away from me particularly.
I've never had a reason to be
Anything but harmless. I saw you coming
Across the yard to the stables; fortunately
The Hungarians were too concerned with themselves
To notice.

GETTNER. What have they come back for?

STEFAN. Not for you.

GETTNER. I didn't think so. But I suppose
Something brought them.

STEFAN. Apparently they've come
To lick their wounds. They had a surprise encounter
With a wandering regiment of Austrian Dragoons,
Not the battle either of them was expecting.
They rounded a corner and came face to face
And were startled into a fight. They hurt each other
And both sides have retired to look it up
In Heister's *Tactics and Military Manœuvre.*

GETTNER. How long do they think they're going to stay here?
How long do you think a man can bear
To be shot through the head by every slamming door he hears?

Purgatory, why do they have to choose
This place to come to?

STEFAN. At your invitation.
I should say it's a natural choice
Since this house became a pocket of the war.
They have a good many wounded, and some dead.
But Peter isn't one of them, if that
Should interest you.

GETTNER. That's something I don't need
To take the blame for. What else is on your mind?
I should suppose no dog-like devotion
Made you follow me in here.

STEFAN. I have to see you
To believe you. How else can I imagine
A man so without benefit to anybody?

GETTNER. Ah, yes; how? How indeed? Or alternatively
I can sleep and dream dreams of good sense
And wake to find the world is past belief.
Either way, imagination's useless.

STEFAN. I wish you would give me the cue for peace.
Maybe I've a lazy temper; certainly
I dislike disliking. You just have to show me
Where you keep your sympathy
For the people I've most affection for,
And I'll understand if I can. How much
Do you care for my mother?

GETTNER. There's no one on earth
I would put to more trouble.

STEFAN. You're succeeding. Already
Her house and her quiet have gone. You set
Great store by your life. What secret value has it
Which makes you claim so much for keeping it?

GETTNER. Unless I live, how do you think I can know?

STEFAN. Suppose its value should be the chance to die
At the right moment?

GETTNER. That's an assumption
Very difficult afterwards to verify.

STEFAN. But if I ever thought we should give you up
I don't think so now. Whole armies might dissolve
For the same reason, but even so, if you honestly
Change step in your mind, I fail to see
How to condemn you. But was it honestly?
Or are my family suffering to let you play?
I have to know before I can be at all easy;
So to make the matter clear would you be ready
To risk your life if I give you the opportunity?

GETTNER. I don't know what the hell you're talking about.

STEFAN. I won't stand to see my family
Made miserable to save a coward, if a coward
Is what you are. You'd honour yourself and me
By exchanging shots at twenty paces.

GETTNER. Should I so?
I'll honour myself by continuing to live,
And honour you by hoping you live indefinitely.

STEFAN. My chance of killing you would be infinitesimal.
I'm no great shot.

GETTNER. Don't be an idiot.
How shall I add to the pleasures of your family
By waving a pistol at you? My boy, you think
Too poorly of me. I would never
Trouble a soul beyond my own small needs.
And I possess enough honour, I might say,

To remain dishonoured without indignation.—
Who's that?

Enter GELDA.

STEFAN. You caught him on the nerve.

GELDA. Poor Richard; we breathed again too soon.
Poor Richard; but none of us can feel
Much favoured by the event. God bless
My grandfather, who thought no building made
By human hands could be too good for horses.

STEFAN. Why, particularly?

GELDA. Because here we have to make
Our home until the Hungarians go. The house
Is hospital, headquarters, barracks,
Armoury, pandemonium.
In the middle of the swarm, immovable
As a queen bee, our mother is standing
Fascinated and appalled.
When I speak she stares at me a moment
As though she couldn't grasp what language I spoke in,
And then turns away, and sometimes
Gasps and claps her hands
Like a little girl at a circus. Do
Bring her away, Stefan. You might persuade her.
I think without knowing it she may break her heart.

STEFAN. I think she may.

[*Exit* STEFAN.

GELDA. Where will you go to be safe?

GETTNER. The possibilities aren't many. Where else
Except here in the loft?

GELDA. It can't be for long:
Perhaps a day.

GETTNER. Not long: perhaps a day!
Only a child could think tomorrow
As far off as it seems to me.
But a child can sleep, and I can court
Insensibility. It is a splendid mercy
The mind needn't be naked for too long.

GELDA. And not feel the naked world, or who
Goes through it. It is a way, certainly.
You made such an outcry about life yesterday
I thought you meant more than undisturbed breathing.
But as I've never been in fear of death
I've no right to question what you do.

GETTNER. No, none;
Though I can tell you, fear as an experience
Is remarkably unenlightening.
What does your young brother mean to do?

GELDA. What should he do?

GETTNER. You perfect and upright family.
I'll go to my wallow where the apples are rotten.

[*He begins to climb the ladder to the loft. He puts his forehead against a rung.*

I don't trust him.

GELDA. No, why should you?
Why should you trust anyone? It's unlikely
You can draw from the world what you never paid into it.
Some people doubt most what they lack most.
Are we to trust you, is my mother to trust you
To keep her from harm?

GETTNER. No, by God, she's beyond harm.
And I'm beyond help, I remember you said.
But my simple nature asks better of men
Than I should ever presume to provide.

GELDA. So far
Wouldn't you say we've answered you? With a shade
Of suffering.

GETTNER. You have. Your mother
Pitched the night on a heroic level.
But now we have come to the drudgery of heroism.
So far you've spoken. But now's the time
When you have to drag out the plain length
Of your magnificent word. I'm only wondering.
The good husband is still among us.

GELDA. Yes,
I know. We've been given the chance to think again.

GETTNER. I'm interested, naturally.
We have to be prepared; first thoughts
Have shallow roots, I imagine.

GELDA. Be reassured.
It's also Peter's wish we should keep you safe.

GETTNER. Is it, by Peter? Then, by Peter, he shows
A very praiseworthy nobility.
And you? You will hardly think the bargain bearable.
You're deeply regretting it.

GELDA. I think neither
Of deep regrets nor of no regrets. You
Are the only gainer, Richard, so be grateful.

GETTNER. Isn't a man to know the reason
For his salvation? I give my gratitude
To what I understand. You wouldn't endure
Being praised for what, after all, may be
A whim of the moment. Come, now, Gelda;
I've some hours to spend in solitary thought,

And I should be happier if all the devil doubts
Could be exorcised.

GELDA. Very well, I'll tell you.
I was a failure to you once. I know
No more about that than I did. But now
In the simpler matter of guarding you
I shall try not to fail.

GETTNER. Is there another
Word in the language so unnecessary
As 'fail' or 'failure'?
No one has ever failed to fail in the end:
And for the very evident reason
That we're made in no fit proportion
To the universal occasion; which, as all
Children, poets, and myth-makers know,
Was made to be inhabited
By giants, fiends, and angels of such size
The whole volume of human generations
Could be cupped in their hands;
And very ludicrous it is to see us,
With no more than enough spirit to pray with,
If as much, swarming under gigantic
Stars and spaces. In this insecure
Situation, I found from the first,
Your mother managed to find a stability
Beside which any despair was compelled to hesitate:
And I was half caught in an expectation of life
Which she was good enough to show no sign
Of expecting from me.
But then—in the way a good hostess
Brings to your notice a fine possession
Without precisely pointing to it—

She made me aware of you;
And to root myself in her radiance
I married you. What did she mean by it?
It was the kind of mockery I knew
So well.

GELDA. Why do you say that? Who mocked you?

GETTNER. You may remember I tried to handle
My native language; in the vain belief
It would give way to me and let me
Turn it to my uses.

GELDA. No one mocked you then.

GETTNER. Reality itself, with wonder and power,
Calls for the sound of great spirits
And mocks us with a wretched human capacity.
Each day has shone full on me. I have senses,
Nerves, and mind. Out of this conjunction
One would suppose there might be born
Words nearly like the world. Yet no;
I wrote frustration syllable by syllable.—
I beg your pardon, it was you
We were talking about. There you were,
Rambling your way out of childhood,
Not knowing what innocence was, being innocent,
And, in a way, perfect in your imperfection.
I don't know how I was expected
To pair with that, unless I was willing
To be the misfortune around the house,
The disappointer of expectations,
Affecting virtue so that I should not see
The shadow go across you.
I preferred to remain unracked, as I preferred
To stay silent, since it wasn't for me

To recreate one word fit to stand
Beside reality, unhumiliated.
And therefore, with mockery refused,
Failure hardly presents itself.

GELDA. Yours may not, but mine may. I meant
To love you. Moreover, I meant I should be loved.
Solemnly to God I said so.

GETTNER. Quite so.
But when promises are merely hopes, and hopes
Aren't realized, where are the promises kept?

GELDA. In me, it would seem.

GETTNER. I see. And I see as well
Strange possibilities.

GELDA. You needn't think
I shall take less care for your safety than I would
If I were still your wife.

GETTNER. You can now tell me
Why you talk to me like this? With no
Confidence at all, I'm bound to ask you
Am I loved in any way? I know I'm not,
But, for my own good, I should like
This conversation well defined.

GELDA. Richard,
There's no definition. I was turning back
To some old thoughts. Some sort of love there was,
But whether it left me or whether I turned from it
It became remote. Sometimes
You can watch a single bird flying over
Towards the vague mountains, until you no longer know
Whether you see or imagine where it is.
I have a feeling of no definition.

GETTNER. I am a man to be loved, is in her mind;
God listen to that, a man to be loved,
She almost says so, as a general theory.
In a world of exact and well-founded husbands
Gettner appears wifeworthy. Be very careful
Or you'll have me wooing my way backwards
To the chancel of All Angels 1838.—
To return you fair for fair,
Now that you're a woman of uncertain mind,
For whom sin and virtue are both
Equally undefinable, I see
You might be loved, more than sufferably.
With the greatest respect, I entertain you
As husbandworthy.

GELDA. If what I said
Turns into that for you, it wasn't worth saying.
I meant that you should lie in hiding
Not altogether alone with fear, and have
A faith in faith, of some sort. But I know
Foreign tongues are as many as human beings
And not easy to translate. Whatever I said
Can be forgotten.

GETTNER. No phrase makes memory
More certain. I like this language, full
Of yes-no and no-yes, and a faith
Which I'm to have and not to have, and things
Which have been but not yet. It belongs
To the origins and life of sense;
All my senses tremble. But if you think
Silence is the better speech
We can kiss without a word,

A dead husband and a dead wife
Perpetuated in a sacrament.

GELDA. The dead may have a thought, but no more deeds.

GETTNER. Now which of us has the fear?
You may have withdrawn the words, but they implied
A kindness which you can't help leaving with me,
Which has to be confirmed. My curiosity
Is great; I begin to wonder who you are.

[He kisses her.

How dead are the husband and the wife? No words, now.
And yet I also wonder how it must feel
To be so close to a living body
Which in a question of hours may well
Be dead, gone, and promising to be rotten?

GELDA. Why won't you be fair? You cheat and cheat.
Be good to me.

[They kiss again, and stand apart.

GETTNER. You were quite right to remember
I married you. It was time I should be reminded.

GELDA. Was it?

GETTNER. The human arms can seem
A great security, for the time they hold.
Pathetically, since they secure nothing.
Nevertheless, it was what you meant.

GELDA. Nevertheless, it could perhaps have been what I meant.

GETTNER. I'm extremely grateful.

Enter STEFAN.

STEFAN. Gettner, if you still
Want to save yourself for better things,
Make yourself scarce. The Hungarians are coming,

Or at least three of them,
And my mother and the Colonel close behind.
The house is given up; you may as well
Be kept. Trouble had better have a cause.

GELDA. Thank you, Stefan.

STEFAN. Did you think I wouldn't warn you?

GELDA. Why, no, but—

STEFAN. Have you really any reason to thank me?

GETTNER [*climbing the ladder*].
Ask him what better thing it is he thinks
I should save myself for? Put it to him.

GELDA. For your own sake is enough.

GETTER [*looking from the loft*]. Don't let me starve.

GELDA. We're not likely to forget you.—Nor remember
Too much the worst of him, Stefan. What was it
He meant me to ask you?

STEFAN. I was hoping
For the best of him. But it's something I haven't got
An answer to, not yet; though I still may get one.

[*Enter* BELLA *and* WILLI *with supplies, and* HUNGARIAN SOLDIERS *carrying furniture.*

[*Exit* STEFAN.

BELLA. You so much as graze it, you'll carry the mark the rest of your life. And choose what you grumble at. You've never been so near to glory as being allowed to have that in your hands, you poor brute creatures, let me say.

1ST SOLDIER. Put it down, Gyuri. She's swearing at us. March all night in the flaking snow, fight all morning in the flaking snow, and then go on fatigues and not flaking grumble. Don't be ridiculous.

BELLA. You can't tell the difference between good and bad. You give your eyes to this, now; it was made many, many years ago with wonderful love and care.

1ST S. So was I, but who's carrying me?

BELLA. I won't waste my time. No, Willi, wipe those tears off your face. Haven't you seen madam is laughing, though never so sad in her life?

WILLI. I want to be a soldier, mam.

BELLA. What, a soldier like these bad men? Bad, abominable men.

2ND S. That's all right, ma. You just tell us what to do before we go and sit down.

3RD S. Make the most of your attitudes. Here's god almighty.

1ST S. Tell him we're not wanting anything.

BELLA. And madam homeless.

[*Enter the* COUNTESS *and* COLONEL JANIK. *The* SOLDIERS *salute.*

COUNTESS. You shall see, Colonel, it is only a little hardship.
You may put me out of your mind, as you put me out of my house:
I shall find employment.

JANIK. Continue, men.

3RD S. Sir.

BELLA. Don't be dismayed, madam. I promise you
They shall handle each thing as though it was myself.

1ST S. Disaster.

JANIK. Get on with your work.

1ST S. Sir!

COUNTESS. And the good soldiers, Bella, take care of them.
They're being put to so much trouble.

BELLA. Who started it, madam?

[*Exeunt* BELLA, SOLDIERS, *and* WILLI.

COUNTESS. A lot of time would be wasted
Going back through the years to answer that.
We could scarcely be of our own time if we would,
Being moved about by such very old disturbances.
If we could wake each morning with no memory
Of living before we went to sleep, we might
Arrive at a faultless day, once in a great many.
But the hardest frost of a year
Will not arrest the growing world
As blame and the memory of wrong will do.

JANIK. Then you have no thought for the downtrodden men,
The overlong injustice, madam?

COUNTESS. Not
As they are downtrodden, but as they are men
I think of them, as they should think of those
Who oppress them. We gain so little by the change
When the downtrodden in their turn tread down.
But then, deserters all, we should all change sides,
I dare say; and that would be proper behaviour
For a changeable world, and no more tiring
Than to go to the extraordinary lengths
Which men will go to, to be identical
Each day. I'm not sure, Colonel, whether I think
Of you as a foe or a friend.
You put me under pain of enmity
And have driven me out of my possessions,
And yet this exile, though it is
No more than a stable-yard from home,

Unites me with you, and with your soldiers
Who are so willing to die
For what death will take away from them.
You teach me to let the world go, Colonel.
I've known this house so long,
Loved it so well
The hours, as they came and went, were my own people.
In obedience, time never failed me, as though
The keys of the year were on my chatelaine.
Summer would end, surely, but the year fell
For my sake, dying the golden death
As though it were the game to put
Hands over my eyes and part them suddenly
When primroses and violets lay
Like raindrops on a leaf
In the beginning of Spring.
The years occupied themselves about me.
The house was perpetual; it was the stars
Which turned and fled. You see how well you have done
To remind me my only privilege
Was to go about a vanishing garden.

JANIK. Countess, madam, you will excuse me;
But I'll kiss your hand, if I may;
Countess, for God's sake, if you'll permit me.

GELDA. Can you ask that, Colonel, ask for a kindness
While you still mean to be unkind?

COUNTESS. To one as poorly circumstanced as I am
It is most considerate and friendly.

[JANIK *kisses her hand.*

Now, I am sure, you must go back to your mischief.

JANIK. It may seem to you a poor sort of divided man
Who stops to apologize in the course of action;

But apology isn't repentance. I have to find
A new heart for these men, in a few hours.
They have ahead of them a day
When their spirit will be worth a nation.
To take your house is bully's work, certainly,
But it has a slight flavour of victory for them
To offset the day's mishap. And two or three
May die tonight more of a Christian death
For the blessing of a roof. You gave
A thousand bodies unexpected comfort
When you put yourself at odds with us yesterday.

COUNTESS. Then I give it again, voluntarily.
But if my behaviour gave you this, then so
Did Richard Gettner's. You will have to acknowledge
The real provoker of your good. Desertion,
As you generously admit, has now
Changed into benefit. You will want to give
Richard Gettner his liberty to do
More good with.

JANIK. That, madam, is woman's logic.
The facts are exactly as they were.

COUNTESS. Facts? Bones, Colonel. The skeleton
I've seen dangling in the School of Anatomy
Is made of facts. But any one of the students
Makes the skeleton look like a perfect stranger.
Richard's fact, in your military law,
Is guilty of death. But Richard's reality
Is making its own way on its own ground,
And only *seems* to take its place in your war.
You can think he is executed already
And entered already into a future life
As a civilian.

JANIK. It passes my understanding
What you imagine you champion in this man?
I see no hope of any outcome
Except the disturbing of your own peace.

COUNTESS. Life has a hope of him
Or he would never have lived. Colonel,
Can you prophesy the outcome of your war?
Yet you still go about it. Richard lives
In his own right, Colonel, not in yours
Or mine.

JANIK. I've said I don't intend
To search for him; but keep him out of my way.

COUNTESS. I shall do what I can to help you.
And then my son-in-law, am I not to see him?
Will he not visit me in exile?

JANIK. You make
Light of the ways of war, Countess.

COUNTESS. I take them
Seriously. And therefore I suppose them
Reasonable, sensible, and civilized.
And therefore I cannot see
Why I should not be allowed to speak to my son-in-law.

JANIK. Well, you shall. I'll send him to you.
But his guard will stay beside him.

COUNTESS. Thank you, Colonel.
We shall give you no trouble. We shall be as you trust us.

[JANIK *salutes and goes.*

I hope I'm not a distraction to providence,
But I seem to be almost undoing
The events of yesterday.

GELDA. Almost
Is a far cry.

COUNTESS. What would you wish to do?
Never to have known the events of yesterday,
Or to have used them differently?

GELDA. For your sake,
Remembering this outcome, never to have known them.
For Peter's sake, never to have known them.
For Richard's sake, could I have used them differently?
For my sake—I don't know how to answer.
Questions I've not known I was asking
Have appeared in fact, as though I called them.

COUNTESS. You've never in all these years questioned
Why I didn't protect you from marrying Richard.

GELDA [*glancing at the loft*].
No. No, I haven't questioned it.

COUNTESS. I sometimes wished you would. Haven't you
Sometimes thought I took no care of you?

GELDA. It was long ago; we won't think of it now.
I wanted to marry Richard.

COUNTESS. There was then
The glow still about him, from having been
The momentary genius of the day,
And there he was unclaimed and difficult,
Charming to a little girl. And there was I
Who guessed it wouldn't be easy.

GELDA. Please don't talk of it now.

COUNTESS. I let you
Marry Richard, though I knew you would find
Happiness only by a fine shade,
Or in some special sense of happiness,

Or not at all. But whoever you had chosen
I couldn't be sure they would cherish you:
And I knew you were prepared that loving Richard
Might be a heavy devotion and a long
Experience of daring. That seemed your purpose;
And I had a pride to see you go
To such a task of love. I knew
Richard was no brute, and no
Pursuer of evil, but more like one enraged
Because he thought that good rejected him.
Or as if an instrument were lying
Thrummed by the wind, refusing any hands
Which might molest the strings into a true sound.

[GETTNER *laughs in the loft. The* COUNTESS *hears him, and raises her voice a little.*

Richard sometimes reminds me of an unhappy
Gentleman, who comes to the shore
Of a January sea, heroically
Strips to swim, and then seems powerless
To advance or retire, either to take the shock
Of the water or to immerse himself again
In his warm clothes, and so stands cursing
The sea, the air, the season, anything
Except himself, as blue as a plucked goose.
It would be very well if he would one day
Plunge, or dress himself again.

GELDA. That isn't the parable to comfort us
On a winter night!

Enter BELMANN *and* JAKOB *carrying a picture.*

COUNTESS. I shall find my spirits again.
Here we are, bringing western culture to the horses.
I've never colonized before.

BELMANN. I should like it
To be understood that by helping Jakob to carry
This picture I haven't agreed with him in the least
About its merits. He is carrying it
To protect it from possible destruction.
I am carrying it to protect the soldiers
From certain corruption of taste. Where
Is the darkest corner?

JAKOB. I sometimes think
His critical judgement is so exquisite
It leaves us nothing to admire except his opinion.
He should take into account
The creative value of the fault.

Enter STEFAN.

BELMANN. Hey, hi, ho! You astonish me.
When I made that precise point yesterday,
You found it such a blinding blow to your honour
You had to challenge me.

JAKOB. A personal matter.
You haven't the right to mention it here.

COUNTESS. I think he should be allowed to mention it;
It may be interesting.

JAKOB. No, really, I must refuse—

BELMANN. It redounds to his credit, and concerns you, Countess.

COUNTESS. So you see, it is interesting.

BELMANN. I said in your absence,
There were things you had done which were arguably
Reprehensible.

COUNTESS. You showed yourself
A master of the obvious. And Jakob

Rightly challenged you for describing me
With such little wit. If his rapier has
No better point, Jakob, you can receive it
On a wide front, and come back to play patience with me.

STEFAN [*to* JAKOB]. Did you really challenge him for that?

JAKOB. As a matter of fact, I'm very worried
About the whole affair.

BELMANN. Ah! You have only
To say so, my dear fellow, I shall excuse you.

JAKOB. I'm not climbing down, nothing of the sort.
What was a point of honour yesterday
Is, of course, a point of honour today.
My concern is that if I should have the misfortune
To kill you—

BELMANN. My concern, surely?

JAKOB. But what faith do you possess, to regard your death
In the light of? Just suppose this affair
Should deliver you up, like a deserter, to
An eternity of reparation?
It kept me awake last night.

BELMANN. Very civil of you.
So perhaps you would like to withdraw?

JAKOB. No,
I should not like to withdraw. It's very
Annoying of you to suggest I should.
But you can assure me first, you're not entirely
Unaware of your soul's journey.

BELMANN. I can't
Assure you. You're being quite impossible.
Now when I tell you I've no particular
Belief in my immortal soul

You will say I'm glad of the excuse
To avoid defending my integrity.
And if, to quieten your scruples, I assume
The appearance of faith, I shall have no integrity
To defend.

JAKOB. That's perfectly true.

BELMANN. And I shall say
You've thought of this for no better reason
Than to get out of the whole affair.

JAKOB. It's not so!
I deny that, absolutely.

COUNTESS. I can see
Nothing will ever happen to either of you.

Enter PETER, *with* TWO HUNGARIAN GUARDS.

GELDA. Peter!

STEFAN. Peter, they swore to me
You were unhurt.

PETER. As they think of wounds,
I am. And I brought this on myself.
In the fight with the Austrian dragoons this morning
I became the very passion I opposed, and was glad to be.
I borrowed a sword out of someone's useless hand,
And as long as the fighting lasted
I was, heart and soul, the revolution.
Janik thought he had won me over,
But on the way back I convinced him otherwise.

STEFAN. You fought for them? I don't understand.
I've never known you to waver yet.

PETER. I suppose
There's no balance without the possibility
Of overbalancing.

STEFAN. What shall we do?
How are we going to set you free of them?

1ST GUARD. We don't stand by for any such talk as that.

COUNTESS. No, you shall not; but you shall sit by me
And have any talk you choose. Are you
Military by nature or misfortune?

1ST GUARD. Well, ma'am—

2ND GUARD. Better say nature. You've heard of nature.
It's us, Rusti.

PETER. It isn't so easy, Stefan.
I don't know at the moment how I can want
To be free of these fellows. I'm no less convinced
Than I always was, they're doing themselves a wrong,
And doing as great a damage to Hungary
As to Austria. But I know it now
In a different sense. I can taste it
Like a fault of my own, which is not the same
Flavour as the fault of some other man.
Besides, I know already from today's showing
That when they fail,
If they do fail and head for defeat,
Being in the heart of their disaster
Makes it more difficult to leave them.
It's an odd chance, Rosmarin,
But your fetching Gettner in
Has faced me with a knowledge I was lacking,
Which in a way has altered nothing
And altered it thoroughly.

BELMANN. May I venture to point out to you, Jakob,
The truth of what I was saying yesterday?
How, as I said, how apparently

Undemandingly the Countess moves among us:
And yet lives make and unmake themselves
In her neighbourhood as nowhere else.

COUNTESS. If, as well as turning a fine phrase,
You also spoke the truth, how proud of you
We all should be.

BELMANN. Thank you my dear Countess.
Yet I'll wager you, Jakob:
One man the Countess will never change
By her divine non-interference:
Ten kronen against Gettner's chances.

JAKOB. Your stable behaviour, I imagine.

COUNTESS. We're continually coming together, as though to live
Pleasantly in one another's conversation,
And each time we find ourselves distracted
By what is happening to us. Do let us
For a short while abandon incident
And charm ourselves with something quite immaterial.

1ST GUARD. I don't know whether you would be interested,
Ma'am, to see a letter from my wife?

COUNTESS. Yes, indeed. How kind of you to show me,
And how the handwriting puts mine entirely to shame.

1ST GUARD. I can't say whose that would be, ma'am.
But you see at the bottom it says 'Your dear wife Anna'.
Those would be her own words, ma'am.
[GETTNER *starts to climb down the ladder from the loft.*

BELMANN. I won't even turn my eyes in the direction
Of what I've seen. No one can say
I'm responsible for anything that follows.

JAKOB. If it's faith you're discussing—

BELMANN. It isn't. No one can say I made any indication.
I'm not responsible for anything that follows.

GELDA [*whispering urgently at the foot of the ladder*].
Go back, go back, Richard!

JAKOB. Gettner!

1ST GUARD. Who's this, then? By jankers, I see who it is!

2ND GUARD. By jankers, do you see who it is?

COUNTESS. Jump
To no conclusions. There's no haste for judgement.
We can make up our minds over a number of years.

1ST GUARD. We've something we know what to do, here.

PETER. Your Colonel
Made a different bargain, Corporal.

COUNTESS. What has brought you to us, Richard?

GETTNER [*full of drink, but carrying it very fairly*].
I was ignored up there. You can ignore
A man till he won't stand it, for anything.
Put him to bed in the dark, at the top of the house,
And tell the lady in the black jet
He's a very difficult child. It's all black jet
As far as your mind can penetrate. I'm a man
Who will dare anything for a ha'penny night-light.

1ST GUARD. They've been looking for you, Captain Gettner.

GETTNER. What shall we say to them, Rusti? Whatever you suggest.

1ST GUARD. You're in serious trouble, sir. You've done it now.
You've made the mistake, God rest your soul.

GETTNER. You forestall me, you rascal Rusti.
If not, what do you mean by addressing the dead
With your hat on? I came to see my wife.

When there's trouble going on, and you know it,
And they won't let you out of the cage,
You fret until you don't know what you do.
You know family trouble, Rusti.

1ST GUARD. Well, sir . . .

STEFAN. What's he doing?

GETTNER. Three incorrigible;
Three incorrigible traitors, can't help it:
The heart, that's one, the brain, that's the second,
And the will, old will power, deserters to the death.
Shoot me now, and tomorrow you can join me.
My wife has married another man.

STEFAN. Heaven's name,
You won't let him go on, Peter.

1ST GUARD. Well, I see
There's no pleasure in that, sir.

PETER. The simple truth
In a way, Stefan. If he can drink himself
To safety, let him.

2ND GUARD [*to the* 1ST]. He's making trouble for us.
If we keep with orders we know we're in the good.

GETTNER. Very sensible; keep to holy writ.
The good sheep give no trouble going to market.
I see your soul shining out in your buttons.
You're a good, right-thinking soldier, Beppy.
I must shake you by the hand, where is it?
Let me shake you by the hand, virtuous fellow.
You make sure I'm shot today, and join me
When they command the last breath out of you.

2ND GUARD. I'll knock stars into anybody
Who says I'm virtuous, and you can charge me.

GETTNER. Don't be sad, Beppy. No tears for me
And I promise there shall be no tears for you.
Don't let a difficult child who's lost his wife
Get in the way of promotion. And before
You die, Beppy, though I hope you live
To be very obedient for several weeks yet,
Say to yourself when you look at the stripe on your arm,
'Here's the last will and testament of Captain Gettner.'

2ND GUARD. I don't know why you have to choose
To walk into us, and in front of witnesses.

COUNTESS. None of us can be called a witness. There are times
When our very so-so vision can rescue itself
Only by failing altogether. I am sure
Neither of you wish to arrest him, and I
Have given my word to the Colonel that Captain Gettner
Shall not be allowed to cross his path. You had better
Undo your collars and sit down again.

1ST GUARD. But, ma'am—

COUNTESS. And I hope if Captain Gettner
Can't be persuaded to stay in hiding, he will help us
By being only apparently among us.
And I would say to him if he were here
That I have given my word to the Colonel also
There should be no offence to him tonight
If we all met together. And no offence—
This is my own promise to myself—
No offence to men who ask no questions
Of their endurance, but endure to live
As these men do. If he were here
I should beg him to remember that.

GETTNER. What did I tell you? Or if I didn't tell you
I tell you: Never come up to expectations,

They'll expect again, and quite differently.
They tell you to be a man of decision,
To take the cold sea in a courageous plunge,
And when you do they squint at you for a fool.
It's the ontological feminine principle.
God's a woman. That surprises you,
But it's perfectly evident in every aspect
Of the arrangement. Create you to think
You're the beloved of God, the blest
Pair of you in a confederation of longing,
With the whispers hot in your ear: Immortal man,
Immortal man achieve me.—And then
You're made another generation of:
The frank daylight's turned full on you,
And her finger withers you with scorn.

BELMANN. Gettner, go and tell your troubles to the Colonel,
Or, if you're staying, try and be tolerable.

GETTNER. I've no troubles; I mislead you.
I have a very interesting wife
Who, for the turn of a leaf, would love me.
Dear slug, she said, I'll be your faith. And so
She is, and here she is. Penelope's
Her name. I'll embrace her in open court
And you all can see the truth of it.

COUNTESS. The truth
Will find its own time of authority, Richard.
It needs no demonstration.

PETER. Gettner,
We can't make any accurate judgement of you
Until you're sober. But that's my last
Excuse for you. Move away from Gelda.

GETTNER [*to* GELDA]. Let me kiss you, or else they'll laugh at me.
[GELDA *makes no move*. GETTNER *kisses her*.

PETER. Extortion by pathos is a poor business,
Gettner. So it would be to use my hands
On a man who only half knows what he's doing.
But a man who mistakes his way can expect to be shown
The road. If you're not quiet now
I'll see you will be.

GETTNER. You're very sure
Which is the mistaken man. Strange world,
If the worthy don't get all the prizes,
I agree, dear fellow; and I'm very sorry
You should ever taste failure, on my word
It's a shame; but Gelda remembers she once married me,
And has an idea to love me. That seems reason
Enough to kiss her in the sight of this congregation,
Without disrespect to anybody.

STEFAN. No, it's not true: you're lying!

GETTNER. Well, of course
That should really be the answer; Gettner's lying.
But then we have a beloved truth with us
Waiting to bear out what I say. Are you
Afraid to ask her, Zichy?

PETER. I'm afraid to guess
How much deeper we shall have to sink
Before we find your lowest mark. But now,
For the time, we won't go lower than we are.
This can rest.

STEFAN. Gelda, why don't you deny it?

PETER. I said it can rest. The man's in the mood
For a brawl in the street. But we won't
Give him satisfaction here.

GETTNER. Satisfaction,
O God, satisfaction.

GELDA. I think I told him so.

STEFAN. You think!

GELDA. I told him so.

PETER. It could be. I can see it could be.

BELMANN. Man, you know him.
For goodness' sake, what do his tricks amount to?
He can't touch you.

PETER. No, no, nothing
Essential.

JAKOB [*to* GETTNER]. Have you now made peace with yourself?

GETTNER. Can't keep things how they should be.
Well, I know I'm drunk.

COUNTESS. How shall we manage, with time at a standstill?
We can't go back to where nothing has been said;
And no heart is served, caught in a moment
Which has frozen. Since no words will set us free—
Not at least now, until we can persuade
Our thoughts to move—
Music would unground us best,
As a tide in the dark comes to boats at anchor
And they begin to dance. My father told me
How he went late one night, a night
Of some Hungarian anxiety,
To the Golden Bull at Buda, and there he found
The President of your House of Deputies
Alone and dancing in his shirtsleeves
To the music of the band, himself
Put far away, bewitched completely
By the dance's custom; and so it went on,

While my father drank and talked with friends,
Three or four hours without a pause:
This weighty man of seventy, whose whole
Recognition of the world about him
During those hours, was when occasionally
He turned his eyes to the gipsy leader
And the music changed, out of a comprehension
As wordless as the music.
It was dancing that came up out of the earth
To take the old man's part against anxiety.

1ST GUARD. That's so, ma'am; I've known my village
(Mindszent, I come from) on best occasions
Dance over the church clock striking
Till so dark you couldn't know
Where your feet would meet the ground
And not give over till the dusk of morning.

2ND GUARD. Rusti's the fellow to do it for you, ma'am.

1ST GUARD. What are you saying? I make a kick and go lifeless
If the music doesn't manage me.

[2ND GUARD *plays a few notes on a mouth-organ.*

COUNTESS. Yes, you must give him the music; I'm sure it will manage him.

1ST GUARD. Shall I, ma'am?

COUNTESS. Yes, indeed you shall. Clear a space for him!
Before long we shall all be dancing.

JAKOB. Dear Countess, not I!

BELMANN. Dance? I should never walk again.

[*The* 2ND GUARD *begins to play. The* 1ST GUARD *takes off his belt and pistol-holster and lays it on the ground.*

1ST GUARD [*ready*]. If you want me to try, put it in funeral time.

[*The* 2ND GUARD *slows the rhythm a little. The* 1ST GUARD *begins to dance. When the dance is well and truly going the* 2ND GUARD *puts away the mouth-organ and gives rhythmic shouts while he also takes off his belt and holster and lays it beside the other, and his jacket also, and joins the dance. The* COUNTESS *punctuates the dance with rhythmic clapping, and* JAKOB *follows her.*

STEFAN *makes his way to the holsters, takes out the pistols and puts them in his pockets while everyone's attention is on the dance. He makes his way down to* GETTNER *and half leads, half pushes him a little farther away from the others.*

STEFAN. You'd better come outside with me, Gettner.

GETTNER. What's the matter?

STEFAN. Come outside; I'll tell you
What's the matter.

GETTNER. It's cold outside.
You don't need to tell me anything.
Go to bed somewhere. I'm not interested.

STEFAN. Aren't you interested? Come out.

GETTNER. You
Look after yourself. I'm a peaceable man.

[*Under cover of clapping from the* COUNTESS *and* JAKOB, STEFAN *smacks his hand across* GETTNER'S *face.* GETTNER *sways on his feet.* STEFAN, *when he has made sure that* GETTNER *has lost his temper, backs slowly away, smiling, to a doorway.*

GETTNER. You won't do that. No, no, no, by Christ Almighty.

[*He follows* STEFAN *out.*

The dance comes to an end.

COUNTESS. Good, good. You shall take breath.

[*The* 1ST GUARD *lies full length on the floor.*

JAKOB. What, are you going to ask them to dance again?
Dear Countess, you and I will be dead with exhaustion.

COUNTESS. I want to learn the song they sing,
The song I heard them singing on the march,
The song that led you through the snow, Corporal,
Lie where you are and sing it to me.

2ND GUARD. What song's that?

COUNTESS. Why, a song. Yesterday
You were very fond of it.

1ST GUARD [*singing from the floor*].
'For God and right we raise the cry
To crush our enemies or die,
And grind them with our heel.
With bloody sword we'll smite the foe
And rivers of their blood will flow,
And drench our valiant steel.'

COUNTESS. No, no, Corporal
I learnt that as a child from my governess.
It wasn't that.

2ND GUARD. Do you think the lady means
'Pretty Thomasina'?

[*The* 1ST GUARD *gives a whistle of dismay*

COUNTESS. Perhaps I do.
I shall know when you sing it.

[*The* 1ST GUARD *sings a tune half-heartedly*

It is the one. But yesterday you sang it
As though there were no other song in the world.
What are the words of it?

1ST GUARD. Ma'am, the words aren't special.

COUNTESS. Neither will my singing of them be.
Let me hear them.

1ST GUARD [*sings*]. 'Why so shy, my pretty Thomasina?
Thomasin, O Thomasin,
Once you were so promisin'.'

COUNTESS. Are these positively the words, Corporal?

2ND GUARD. You'd better be obliged for what he gives you, ma'am.

COUNTESS. Very well, I will be. [*Sings.*] 'Why so shy', &c.
And then, Corporal?

1ST GUARD [*Sings*]. I shall woo you on my concertina.
[*Embarrassed.*] La la la la la la la—
[*Triumphantly.*] Thomasin–a!

[*The* COUNTESS *and the* GUARDS *sing the song again. Two pistol shots from outside. The* GUARDS *make a rush for their holsters.*

2ND GUARD. The Austrians, Rusti! They've surprised us!

1ST GUARD. A trap, they've set for us. Who's got our pistols?
Gone blinding into it. Oh, ma'am. What
Did we deserve this for?

2ND GUARD. Who's got our pistols?

COUNTESS. Who has done this to them?

BELMANN. Where is Gettner?

1ST GUARD. That Gettner! We had the chance of him
And let him twist us well and truly.
Now what do we say to them?

2ND GUARD. I said we should keep to orders.

PETER. You have my word
There's no trap. I have an altogether
Different fear.

COUNTESS. Where has Stefan gone?

[GETTNER *appears in the doorway.*

GETTNER. Rosmarin, Rosmarin.

COUNTESS. What are you saying to me?

GETTNER. It was nothing I did. I swear to you,
Rosmarin, I swear to you I aimed
Deliberately wide. I shot
Well wide of him. The boy
Was clear enough where he stood. Something
Turned the bullet. I didn't shoot him.

PETER. What does he mean for God's sake?

1ST GUARD. Stay still. We're here to see you stay.

BELMANN. Well, did you leave him there? Is that
The way to have left him? Wait, Countess, wait:
We'll go.

JAKOB. We'll bring him here to you.

[*Exeunt* BELMANN *and* JAKOB.

COUNTESS. Where is Stefan, Richard?

GETTNER. Why me, why me?
I didn't make the gust of a wind, the tree-trunk,
Or whatever it was killed him. I aimed away.
I was laughing him off, but I heard him fire
And the bullet coming. I did refuse to meet him.
Before God, I said No, I said No, no, no.

COUNTESS. Richard, give me a quiet answer
To what I need to know from you.
You must say to me, Stefan is living.

GETTNER. He made me go with him, he made me mad.
But outside I was sober, outside the mist was clearing;
I aimed away, at a low star. But then

I felt him shoot, and my body jarred
From head to foot, and my pistol fired.

COUNTESS. Then say Stefan is dead. Say to me
I've killed Stefan.

GETTNER. No!

COUNTESS. Is Stefan dead?
All I am asking, Richard,
Is the courage of an answer. Not why;
But whether I go on without him.

Enter KASSEL.

KASSEL. I've come from Stefan, Rosmarin. Belmann
And Jakob tell me you've been given
A wickedly exaggerated account
Of what has happened.

COUNTESS. Exaggerated?

KASSEL. Stefan is alive, Rosmarin.

COUNTESS. You've come to say so, little physician.
I hadn't let him go so easily.

KASSEL. The orderlies will bring him here. Rosmarin,
You must know he is hurt, but, the blessing of being so young,
New life will graft on a thread. By a stroke of luck
I was near when it happened. This precious idiot
Saw Stefan fall and went nowhere near him,
Belted off like a madman, and brought
His hideous farrago of nonsense to you.

1ST GUARD. It's come to this, the Captain's no use
To any of us. If we can get
Our pistols back, we'll take him to the Colonel.

2ND GUARD. Before he lands us in any more trouble.

BELMANN [*in the doorway*].
I second your wisdom, Corporal. He's been
Free too long.

1ST GUARD. That's right.
Back to plain duty. Send him to draw his pay.

COUNTESS. Corporal, have you children?

1ST GUARD. Yes, ma'am, yes.

COUNTESS. Would you injure them, to please any opinion?

1ST GUARD. Ma'am, that's no question.

COUNTESS. Then do not injure
Mine. I mean my son. I ask you
Not to make him the cause of punishment,
Not to make his wound a death,
Not to turn his challenge into a judgement.
The stream of his life is running
Shallow and slowly. Pray for him,
Not because I love him, but because
You are the life you pray for. And because
Richard Gettner is the life you pray for.
And because there is nothing on the earth
Which doesn't happen in your own hearts.
—Richard, let me have your arm to lean on.
My body sometimes tells me
I'm not here for ever.—Richard.

RICHARD *makes no move. Enter* JAKOB.

JAKOB. Dear Countess, Stefan is coming. They're bringing him now.

[*The* COUNTESS *almost falls.* KASSEL *and* JAKOB *support her. They try to lead her to a chair but she puts them aside.*

COUNTESS. No, no, that is over now. Perhaps for a moment
He drew-in a draught of my strength. And now
He comes on again with life, as I do. I can stand,
I can welcome him. I need no help.

THE CURTAIN FALLS

ACT THREE

The staircase, and the room, disfigured by the Hungarian occupation

[GELDA *is staring out of a window.* STEFAN, *in dressing-gown, moves into view upstairs, and* GELDA *hears him.*

GELDA. What is it, Stefan? What do you want? Get back to bed.

STEFAN. I know mother must be very ill.
I'm going to see her.

GELDA. You're going to be well yourself
Before you start on any adventures.

STEFAN. She would have been to see me long before
If she hadn't been very ill.

GELDA. Do you know
How narrowly and recently you've come
Back to us, Stefan? How carefully
You still have to obey us? Go back to bed;
Please, Stefan.

STEFAN. She may be worrying about me;
But if she sees me there beside her
She'll know I'm all right again; we can improve
Together.

GELDA. She will know you should never be there;
You will make it harder for her, not easier,
When she sees you looking more frail and paler
Than she ever dreamt you could. Keeping your bed
Is as much for her sake as for yours, Stefan.

STEFAN. When will she be well again?

GELDA. When you are;
Presently; together you can improve.

STEFAN. All right, but make sure of that. Tell her
How nearly well I am.

Enter BELLA.

BELLA. Whatever is going on?
Does the boy mean to give us more sorrow than ever?
By making himself ill again? We pray
God to keep him, and he makes it as difficult
As can be. I suppose he means us all to go
And cry round his bed when he's worse again.

GELDA. It's all been said, and he understands.
He's going back to his room.

STEFAN [*as he goes*]. Good evening, Bella.

BELLA. He says good evening, as though I should answer
Such wicked people.

GELDA. Are you very good, Bella?
How many days is it since you slept?
My mother says make Bella sleep.

BELLA. I rest
Best when I'm watching over her.
Once I begin to nod it all comes back—
How they've broken this poor house to pieces
And I think of it and I tell myself
It 's no good to worry, what can't be done
Is beyond the angels; and that cause of it,
That Gettner—

GELDA. Richard Gettner has gone away.
You needn't think of him now. Forget him, Bella.

BELLA. What has he ever done good enough to forget?

GELDA. The revolution's over,
I'm sure it's over. The whole of yesterday
We heard the guns, and today there's nothing
But the noise of the rain. All night I was hearing
The scattered solitary horsemen
Galloping down the road; there was no
Dead-march drum of the guns any longer.
I heard the wind, and I heard the hail,
And I heard the hoof-beats, and otherwise
There was peace.

BELLA. There's no
Pleasure in fair weather when the stooks are black:
Except that, now it's over, we shall see
Count Peter coming to take you home.

GELDA. I pray so.
But if I should never see him again
I've made myself into an enemy
I shall never defeat. Bella, he went away
Believing—

[*Hammering at the outside door.*

I think he has come.

BELLA. That may be; you can't tell.

GELDA. Go to the door, Bella. No, no, I shall go.

[*She runs to the door and stops.*

How do I know? It may be someone bringing
News; almost any news.

BELLA. Let me see
What the truth of it is.

GELDA. Well, hurry, then,
And call out to me.

BELLA. If it isn't the best news
I open the door to, there's no hurry
To call out any other.

[*Exit* BELLA.

GELDA [*calling after her*].
If you won't call out, perhaps I shall come with you,—
I don't think I'm ready, I don't think so.

[*She goes to the window.*

The rain;
I wish it would wash the last few days away.

Enter PETER.

Peter! Now you're safely out of it all.

PETER. No one is safely out of it ever.
It goes on, Gelda.

GELDA. I was telling myself it was over.

PETER. I have to go to Vienna.

GELDA. Why, Peter?

PETER. You had to know where I was; that
Was the only reason for coming here.
But I should have been in Vienna long ago.

GELDA. Was that your only reason for coming?

PETER. The Hungarians are broken completely.

GELDA. It was what you were afraid of.

PETER. I was afraid
They'd lose the liberties they were beginning to gain
Lately; not that we should lose the humanity
We took of God two thousand years ago.

GELDA. Peter, what is it?

PETER. The government is shooting and hanging
Every Hungarian of note who fought in the war.
They're holding contemptuous, contemptible
Courts-martial on the field, and executing
Men, one after the other—men
Whose families have given generations
Of service to the Emperor.

GELDA. On whose authority
Can they dare to do this?

PETER. Schwarzenberg's,
In the name of the Emperor. What torments me
Is whether I might not have prevented it
If I'd never left Vienna: whether that ride here,
Whether Stefan's message of alarm for Rosmarin,
Wasn't one cause of these deaths and the endless consequences.
I'm too late, but I have to go there.
And, though I'm too late, every moment here
Makes me feel I'm betraying someone.

GELDA. You have to go; very soon.

PETER. I have to go
Forty-eight hours ago. You can give me
Your prayers for what's already hopeless.
I'll get word to you when I can.

GELDA. Peter!
Shall we say anything about ourselves?

PETER. There's going to be time for that.

GELDA. How do you know there's going to be time?
I know I shall sit here, after you've gone,
Making for myself a hundred accidents
Which would mean I could never talk to you again.
I can see the road to Vienna

A river of drifting, hopeless,
Dangerous men. And then I see myself
Telling myself for the rest of my life
What I should have said to you.

PETER. You make me think
I shall betray something either way,
Staying or going. If I stay, I think
Of nothing but getting to Vienna. If I go,
I think of nothing but what you have said to me.
Say it to me.

GELDA. Now I know it will take
A century to tell you. I could wish
You needed to listen as anxiously
As I need to explain to you.

PETER. In the still of my mind
I do.

GELDA. In the still of my mind
I know I've never done anything to hurt us;
Only in the wandering, so easily cheatable
Part of me, where a right thought—
Or at least an excusable thought—suddenly
Finds it has taken pity on a horde
Of domineering wrong ones. It may have been right,
That first instinct, to put out with a lifeboat
For Richard, but on to it scrambled
Such a crew of pirates, my curiosity,
My pride, my ambition to succeed
Where I failed before, my longing to discover
What conversions could be made by love,
We all began to sink. And it was Stefan
Who rescued me, when he nearly died for the truth;
You and I are the truth.

PETER. If that contents you
It will always content me.

GELDA. I don't know whether
You're hurt or angry.

PETER. Neither; I love you,
But I'm impatient.

GELDA. It would be a wry joke on me
If it were you, not Richard, who turned out
To be the intractable one I had to subdue.
I thought I'd almost brought our world to an end,
But you didn't greatly notice it.

PETER. There have been
Many things in my heart, and you and I
Were not the least of them. But other worlds
Come to an end tonight, Gelda,
More irreparably than ours. That's why
I have to go.

GELDA. And, now I've said my say,
I wish you were there already,
I wish you had ridden straight there without thinking about me.
It must be possible still to make Schwarzenberg
See reason.

PETER. A little late.

Enter JAKOB *and* BELMANN.

BELMANN. Why, Zichy,
How do you manage to be here? Have the Hungarians
Come to grief?

PETER. To grief, certainly.
So have we.

BELMANN. In what way, so have we?

GELDA. Don't keep him now.

JAKOB. Why off so soon?

PETER. We're celebrating victory
By executing every considerable officer
We can lay our hands on. I think someone
Should go and ask them why.

GELDA [*outside the door*]. Hurry, Peter!

PETER. And I'm going to ask them why.

[*Exit* PETER.

BELMANN. So he should. Though the degrees of distinction
Between admirable, permissible, and outrageous slaughter
Haven't yet been made perfectly clear to me.
I understand we should lament an earthquake
And prepare to contrive an earthquake
With equal zest.

JAKOB. It's something to know
The revolution's over. After living
This marooned sort of life for so many days
We can welcome a return to normal.

BELMANN. With Gettner gone, the world does take on
A slightly more encouraging appearance.

Enter KASSEL, *by the lower door.*

JAKOB. Really, out walking, Dr. Kassel, in this terrible weather?

KASSEL. The ostler's wife came to the conclusion
The world could do with another young woman. Not
My place to contradict; though on the face of it
An umbrella would have been more sensible.
If circumstances hadn't seen
I was somewhere handy, old Doctor Brünn would have had
A hard, filthy ride here, through all manner of disaster,
And come into the bedroom (I've seen him do it)

Saying What's all this about, what's all this about?
As though he would deliver the child once
But that would have to be the end of it.

JAKOB. How are they now, the two of them?

KASSEL. The mother's
Pleased with herself; the child can't disguise
An extreme disgust at the whole affair.
Well, they'll come to some working arrangement.—
So the revolution's come to a bad end, they tell me.

BELMANN. Zichy says the Government is making
Examples of them; brute vengeance going on.

KASSEL. Ah, is that so? They're determined the world shall have
Incident; they mean the historians
Never to fail for matter. Don't depress me
Any further.

JAKOB. One always thinks if only
One particular unpleasantness
Could be cleared up, life would become as promising
As always it was promising to be.
But in fact we merely change anxieties.
In a day or two the road to Vienna
Should be clear to take again, but I hardly
Know what to do. No road is clear
Until the Countess is out of danger.

Re-enter GELDA.

KASSEL. There's no chance, I'm afraid, that Rosmarin
Will hold you here much longer.

JAKOB. What are you saying?

BELMANN. Is it so serious? That's difficult to grasp.
You would think she would somehow have taken
The world with her.

JAKOB. Do you really mean
There's no hope, Kassel? No grain of hope?

KASSEL. We can count a day, perhaps: a day or two,
But I can't promise more, even remembering
How well her spirits will always argue
Against the doubts of her body. After that
The hours we have with her will be gifts
Out of the air.

GELDA. I think today she knows it,
And seems willing. At least, suddenly
She wrinkled her forehead, her eyes laughed,
And she raised her hand in the way she does
When she has been convinced by an argument
She completely disapproves of.

BELMANN. Kassel, will you cast your eye? Upward.
Is this in order?

[*The* COUNTESS *is descending the stairs.*

JAKOB. Wonderful!
It's our world revived.

KASSEL. Our world a fool,
I'm sorry to say.

GELDA. Shall I go to her?

KASSEL. Wait a moment, wait a moment.
Her body won't save her; there's no harm in seeing
What comes of a still willing spirit.

BELMANN. She has a great ambition.

JAKOB. A great spirit.

KASSEL [*calling to the* COUNTESS].
Well, Rosmarin, so you've planned
To take us by surprise.

COUNTESS. Now I know why a snail has eyes
Which reach so far in front of him.
He is too impatient to be there.

KASSEL. Would you take my arm, if I come to you?

COUNTESS. No, no;
If you will be patient I will be persistent.
Within my experience there's never been
Anything so precariously promising
Since I first faltered
Five steps into the lap of my grandmother.
Which I can't remember. But great things came of it.

GELDA. Darling, wait to talk until you come to us.

COUNTESS. Ssh!

BELMANN. I don't know when I hung on each moment
In such fascination, unless when I watched
A fishing boat outwit the rocks and a very
Unbenevolent sea. It did at last
Gain the shore.

GELDA. Now, surely, for this last
Easy level, which isn't worth defying,
You can let me take you.

COUNTESS. Well, I will,
And then I can talk again.

JAKOB. Dear Countess,
How welcome you are you can never know.

COUNTESS. I welcome myself, too. It felt as though
You had all fled to the Antipodes.

KASSEL. It's now my business to lecture you, seriously.
While I do, you can be as inattentive

As you always are. But you pay me to give you advice.
And, in the name of my honest profession, I will.

COUNTESS. Little physician, I'll waive your fees
If you'll allow me my own legs,
At least when I need them.
I've been making, in retrospect, some calculations
By the sun, though the sun has been obscure,
And it seems to me today is Thursday!

JAKOB. It is, you know! We overlooked it
With all the anxiety, but today is Thursday!

COUNTESS. And when the last Thursday comes,
Which may be this one, I should like to be present.
So many years of meeting deserve to end
In a rare parting. It's quite true, the world
Being uncertain, I may spoil it all
By being here again next Thursday. But I'd rather
Go out, after the style of a night-light,
In a series of apologetic returns,
Than leave without ceremony, which would be surely
Ungracious to an earth which has entertained me.

KASSEL. Why not spare yourself, Rosmarin, for those returns?
Give to illness the same respectful hearing
I've seen you give to bores and fools.

COUNTESS. Respectful?
I've been reverential. I've heard illness out
Until it has nothing more to say to me,
And I thank God I have the last word.

BELMANN. But that
May be many years away.

COUNTESS. You don't think so,
And I can't think of any praiseworthy reason

Why you should say so. Tell me instead
What is the news of the world I'm leaving?
Where is Richard Gettner?

GELDA. Richard has left.

COUNTESS. Left for where?

GELDA. He didn't say.
A horse has gone from the stables, and Richard
Has also gone.

COUNTESS. Which horse?

GELDA. Xenophon.

JAKOB. Don't be hurt again by that fellow.
Nothing he does is worth a thought.
Now he turns on his heel
After doing you such injury.
Afraid to look at what he's done,
And leaves not one word in compensation.

COUNTESS. I wish he hadn't taken Xenophon.
Xenophon's got a saddle gall.
I hope Richard will notice, and think of him.
But no cure comes by sighing, and I can't
Go off in pursuit, wherever they've gone.
Only, if any of you hear of Richard,
Ask after Xenophon.
We must value this evening as the one
Thursday in the universe, for the rest
Have gone, and no more may come,
And we should be on our most immortal behaviour.
I see that nothing of the sort can be expected.

BELMANN. If it entertains you, if you insist,
We'll make believe this is to be a farewell.

COUNTESS. You're very grudging.

JAKOB. It's impossible!
How can you bear to think of it?

COUNTESS. But you've always thought of it, Jakob,
In the pleasure and conversation of these evenings.
The argument, philosophy, wit, and eloquence
Were all in the light of this end we come to.
Without it there would have been very little
To mention except the weather. Protect me
From a body without death. Such indignity
Would be outcast, like a rock in the sea.
But with death, it can hold
More than time gives it, or the earth shows it.
I can bear to think of this:
I can bear to be this, Jakob,
So long as it bears me. [*Someone taps on a window.*

JAKOB. Who's that? What is it?

COUNTESS. Who can it be?

BELMANN. I see who it is, or who it has been.
If the Hungarians have been smashed, then this
Is an apparition off the battlefield.
What do we do about him? Are you prepared
To entertain another world?

COUNTESS. But, of course,
I'm ready for whoever cares to haunt me,
Though I think a living man will haunt the world
More desperately than anything out of the grave.
Let him in.

[JAKOB *opens the window.* COLONEL JANIK *enters.*

BELMANN. I'm not sure how to address you, Colonel. Are you
Dead or alive?

COUNTESS. Are you ill or distressed,
Colonel? It's alarming to see you.
What are your cares now? And why
Do you come to my window?

[JANIK *cannot trust himself to speak.*

Is it more
Harsh and necessary business
Which if you could you would spare me? Colonel,
First of all say any trivial thing;
We shall come presently to the other.—Child,
I know your cause is lost, but in the heart
Of all right causes is a cause which cannot lose.—
Your men, the men who stood here in the snow,
They fought, Colonel, and they've been destroyed.
Will you tell me?

JANIK. They fought, and nothing 's left.
Who came out of that isn't worth saving.

COUNTESS. You mean yourself.

JANIK. No, madam, I'm not out of it.
None of us who had command
Is to be left alive to think liberty.
By now they know which way I slipped by them:
It won't be long before they're round me in a ring.
But I thought Count Zichy might be here, Countess.
I thought he might let me have one word with him.

GELDA. He came not long ago and left again for Vienna.

JANIK. I came to tell him what Austria does to us.
Excuse me; three times I've used your house
Without civility. I won't again.

COUNTESS. Wait, Colonel. You're the man
Who can help me to remember. There was a song

Your men sang while they were marching, they called it
Pretty Thomasina, and I began to learn
To sing the tune: all today
I've been trying to recall it.
Be so good, Colonel, remind me of it.

JANIK. Be so good, don't ask me for songs now.

COUNTESS. Be so good, you will remember it,
To save me teasing my memory any longer,
You will sing it.

[JANIK *sings a few bars of the tune.*

There it is; that's how it went.
—Colonel, it isn't safe for you to leave here.

BELMANN. Countess, it isn't safe for you to harbour him!

JAKOB. You've given yourself enough suffering already.

JANIK. I've not much wish for safety; and anyway
Nothing I can do is more than a postponement.

COUNTESS. No, no, you will stay here; that's decided.

JANIK. I neither want protection, nor would I ask
To be given it here. I've troubled this house enough.

COUNTESS. Then you won't want to put me to the trouble
Of persuading you, but simply hide yourself.

KASSEL. Rosmarin, nothing you've known will tell you
What you're asking to be faced with.

COUNTESS. They're men still who do this. I'm not faced yet
With hell itself. Away with you, Colonel.
You shall find the turret
By going left and right, and right and left again,
And there at an angle with the corridor

Is a door you will see, not much bigger than a child,
And through it a turning stair to the belfry.

JANIK [*going up the stairs*].
What am I letting you do? You'll find
These men are more determined. There's little chance
It will turn out well.

COUNTESS. My wretched, failing memory!
Do, Colonel, put me in mind of the song again.

[JANIK *sings from the stairs. The* COUNTESS *picks up the song and* JANIK *goes on and out of sight.*

There are better songs, of course.

BELMANN. This is madness.

JAKOB. What do you mean to become of us all?

KASSEL. Rosmarin, I beg you, don't destroy yourself.

BELMANN. Haven't you any fear of consequences?

COUNTESS. There's one thing I'm afraid of.
I've become so absent-minded. My memory,
Desperate perhaps to forget nothing
Of my twenty-thousand days of life,
Is here, there, everywhere, but nowhere long,
Like a bat in a bedroom. So if I should confuse
My nationalities, or seem to be pleading
Richard's defence, instead of the Colonel's,
Do what you can to rescue me.
Say Pipistrello, and I'll draw back.

BELMANN. They may get quickly tired of the argument,
And decide that *we* have qualified for traitors
As well as Janik.

COUNTESS. There is nothing
They may not do; there's no foolishness

They may not think; souls who will not budge
Out of their barren islands.

[*She begins to sing again.*

Enter RICHARD GETTNER.

GETTNER. They said you were dying.

JAKOB. He can't come here!
What's to be done with him?

BELMANN. With your permission,
Countess, we can quite easily
Persuade him to go.

KASSEL. I definitely forbid
Any kind of disturbance.

COUNTESS. Very welcome,
Richard. How is Xenophon?

GETTNER. They said you were dying, or dead. Otherwise
I should never have come from where I was,
Which was nowhere in particular, which suits me,
And nowhere long enough to stale the air
Too fatally. But how this rumour
Got where it did, is beyond all things
Extraordinary. Impossible anyone
Could have overtaken me and gone ahead.
I was going away from you at a full gallop.

COUNTESS. O Xenophon!

GETTNER. And yet every village had the story.
At the first inn I stopped at, the whole family
Came out to me, cousins and the lot,
Catching hold of the bridle and my boots,
Every face as wet as my shoulders.
Did I know you were dying? Was it true,

Were you dying? I told them
Not for another fifty years.
And when I couldn't convince them I pushed on.
But there wasn't to be any riding out of it;
The news had torn up your entire county.
Even the most outlandish hovels
Flung some creature practically under the horse
Shouting to know was it true you were dying.
If you weren't dying you were dead.
In the end I was so sick of the information,
And sick of seeing faces
Plastered with tears and rain, the road became
A nightmare and impassable.
So I turned round, which I now see
Was unnecessary. I should have stuck
To my first incredulity, and ridden
Straight on over the faces.

COUNTESS. And then I should never have known how well
They think of me; anyway how they care
About my leaving them. It makes me feel
Gross and unaccommodating
Not to bear out what they told you, Richard.
But it is a little irksome, always
To live up to the world's opinion in such matters.
I am proud of their tears. Now it will take
A life all over again to deserve them,
And I've hardly got to the end of this one.
Richard, forgive me, I've spoilt your journey,
And you've rewarded me with a great happiness.

GETTNER. Great hypocrite! You know I had no intention
Of giving you pleasure. And I wonder
You like to let your thirst for admiration
Lap up these tears.

COUNTESS. As they were wept for me
It's just as well I am here to appreciate them.

BELMANN. Will someone give me the word to get rid of this man?

JAKOB [*at the same time*].
I can't and won't hold my tongue any longer—

KASSEL. No, no, no, for the sake of our dear friend,
No quarrelling.

BELMANN. Then perhaps Gettner
Will show us how to admire him. There happens
To be the opportunity, Gettner. Upstairs
In the bell-turret, which you may remember,
There's another fugitive hiding now:
Colonel Janik. Convince the Countess, if you can,
To keep this house innocent of any more disasters.

GETTNER. What claim has Janik on this house?
What do you owe to Janik?

COUNTESS. You need have no
Concern, Richard. Colonel Janik hides here.

KASSEL. Rosmarin, unless you mean to distress me,
Let me take you back to your room.

COUNTESS. No, no:
Richard has ridden a great distance to see me;
But I see we're interrupting each other's pleasure.
I suggest that for half an hour or so
We should go about our devices. And my device
Is to be left alone to talk with Richard.

KASSEL. But, Rosmarin, will you remember it's I who carry
The responsibility?

COUNTESS. I've always been willing
As you know, to give you the credit for my health.

But you mustn't monopolize my death also;
That shall be quite my own. You shall come back
In half an hour, and find me
So well, I could go to bed. You must be
As trustful as I am when I take your medicines.
I prescribe you half an hour's absence.

KASSEL. I take it
As you take my medicines, with appalling grimaces.

JAKOB. It goes very much against my heart
To leave you Countess; but since you wish it. . . .

BELMANN. Hardly a day passed in my boyhood
Without someone sending me out of the room.
I'm very well practised in withdrawing
As a matter of course, with the merest hint of surprise.

COUNTESS. It is so useful to have been a child.
Presently I shall long for you all to be with me.

[*Exeunt* KASSEL, JAKOB, *and* BELMANN.

GELDA. Richard, when you took Xenophon and rode away,
Neither you nor I, nor Peter, knew what following time
Was going to make of us. But you rode out
Of the indecision; and so did I. I think,
Mercifully, Peter and I have made our peace.

GETTNER. I'm not insensible of that mercy.

GELDA. I shall go up now and sit with Stefan.
Until the half-hour is over.

COUNTESS. Tell him
I looked in and saw him for a moment
Splendidly sleeping.

GELDA. He may be sleeping still.

[*Exit* GELDA.

GETTNER. So it's true you're ill.

COUNTESS. Oh, Richard, be careful.

GETTNER. What have I said?

COUNTESS. For a moment I thought
You were trying to find words appropriate
To visiting the sick.

GETTNER. Which you would find
Inappropriate and ridiculous.
But they'd be ten times less inappropriate
Than your detestable illness. And it is
Detestable, that you should be one more
Point of bleakness in a time
Already stark with punishment.
You can stoop your eyelids down, and make them
Close on a calm of mind.
But we don't live under your eyelids. There, perhaps,
By a serene elimination of
Three-quarters of the earth, you can exist
Beside the still waters. But out here
The drowning still goes on.

The COUNTESS *rests.*

And I'm the cause
Of this illness, I suppose.

COUNTESS. The arithmetic
Of cause and effect I've never understood.
How many beans make five is an immense
Question, depending on how many
Preliminary beans preceded them.

GETTNER. But you haven't much doubt I brought this on you.
If I'm to be set loose, you shall be caught:

It's in the world's best manner.
The shrug of events, the *quid mihi est*,
So long as the punishment falls
It's inconsequential where.
And you let the cynical will be done, and I'm
To be saddled with the shame of it.
Rosmarin, you can consider this again,
And give up this threat of dying. I see there's to be
No living without you. I think you should marry me.

COUNTESS. I'm not going to ask you why. I shall quietly
Sit and let those astonishing words
Wash over me. They're contenting words
For any woman to have heard
As she goes where she goes. You, Richard!
You, of all men on the earth,
To be the one to say to dying things
'Be a beginning.'
And indeed, please God, to the last moment
I will begin; but not by marrying.

GETTNER. Why not? Why not by marrying?

COUNTESS. It takes
Thought, and my thoughts are crowded. And some
Gravity, and I have an inconsolable
Inclination to laughter. And then, again,
Time: time to formulate,
Winnow, find, and have
A husband.

GETTNER. Now so simple.
You love me, and I want to marry you.

COUNTESS. Tell me, Richard, what complication of logic
Made you think I loved you?

GETTNER. There was never
Anything better demonstrated.
In the mythology of woman with man
Show me a tale more certain, unswayable,
Abundant, and long-suffering, than this
Of you with me.
Jealousy at the top of its fever
Couldn't have found one hesitation
To brood over and magnify.
I acknowledge it.

COUNTESS. Richard, Richard,
What virtue I've missed! If only I'd thought
Of being such a woman while there still
Was time to try! What my memory
Might not have done to future women in love
To charge them with ardours of self-sacrifice,
Half devotees, half nightingales, three-quarters
Idiotic. I'm a fool to deny
What you so beautifully praise me for,
But truth leaps in me, and I have to confess
I haven't loved you.

GETTNER. You mean I haven't behaved
In a way due to receive it.

COUNTESS. I mean, simply,
It never came about.
There we have no free-will.
At the one place of experience
Where we're most at mercy, and where
The decision will alter us to the end of our days,
Our destination is fixed;
We're elected into love.

So, Richard, whosever negligence it is,
I never loved you.

GETTNER. I've nothing to say.
If you say so I can't contradict you.
I imagine it's more than ever satisfactory
To have done so much for a mere liking.

COUNTESS. Don't praise me; I never in my life
Was so unfit for praise. It would have been
Easier to love you than to like you, Richard.

GETTNER. I see you're determined to put me in my place.
You're going to insist on taking your revenge.

COUNTESS. If so, the revenge is on no one but me.
I'm not proud of being so insufficient
That I could like you no more than occasionally.
Just now I was very proud,
Thinking of all the villages in tears,
But I sit reproved,
A small, shameful bundle of prejudice.

GETTNER. You could like me no more than occasionally.
So that's it.

COUNTESS. I'm not worth a thought,
I've put myself beneath your notice.

GETTNER. Will you tell me, then, what I meant to you?
A penance you gave yourself? Was I
An exercise in charity
Which is proving unfortunately fatal?
Isn't it a sort of insolence
To do for me what you care so little about?
What in God's name was it I meant to you?

COUNTESS. Simply what any life may mean.

GETTNER. I see myself reduced to one dimension;
I'm not loved or liked by you. That fairly
Disposes of me. I pity myself.

COUNTESS. We need
Neither of us despair. I'll not
Leave you until I can love you, Richard.

GETTNER. It's no comfort to imagine us
Clasped here indefinitely, anxiously waiting
To love and be loved.

COUNTESS. I don't mean
Necessarily here.

GETTNER. I'm not prepared to wait.
I shall go back to the journey I was making
In no direction in particular,
Where the dark makes no false promises.
I'll borrow, if I may, a fresher horse than Xenophon,
And this time ride through the nightmare and not turn back.
Your days are well rid of me, and so goodnight.

[*Exit.*

The COUNTESS *sings again.*

COUNTESS. There was more to come, so I imagine,
But then they were interrupted.
I wish I could go on singing.
I am very much in love with something;
What it may be I can't remember;
It will come to me.
That was a roundabout drive in the snow,
Owing to my eccentric sense of direction!

[*A hammering on the door.*

[*Re-enter* GETTNER.

GETTNER. They're here, at the door, the Austrians for Janik,
So you will understand if I avoid them

And go this way out to the stables.
You can't sleep now; you've given your word to receive them.
Rosmarin? Aren't you going to face them?
Do you mean this absolute no? Rosmarin.

[*The hammering on the door.* GETTNER *goes to the window and opens it to make his escape. He turns to the* COUNTESS'*s chair.*

You're dead, Rosmarin. Understand that.
What is there to stay for? You never showed
Any expectations of me when you were alive,
Why should you now?
This isn't how I meant that you should love me!

[*He closes the window and comes back to her and speaks curtly.*

Very well, very well. [*He stands beside her.*
Be with me.

[*The hammering on the door.*

Enter BELLA.

BELLA. They must be quiet! How can I send them away
If they will come in?

GETTNER. You can't send them away,
Bella, if they will come in.

BELLA. But Madam—

GETTNER. She knows
They're here. She says yes we're to let them in.
Go to the door, Bella, and let them in.

[*The hammering at the door increases as* BELLA *goes out.*

THE CURTAIN FALLS

Melodies arranged and composed by
Leslie Bridgewater

HUNGARIAN DANCE

PRETTY THOMASINA

PATRIOTIC SONG

CURTMANTLE

A Play

SECOND EDITION

To

JOHN AND NANCY FRY

The play was first produced on 1 March 1961 at the state opening of the Stadsschouwburg, Tilburg, Holland, by the Ensemble Company, directed by Karl Guttmann

World première in English at the Edinburgh Festival, 4 September 1962

London première at the Aldwych Theatre, 6 October 1962, with the following cast:

William Marshal	ROY DOTRICE
Barber	JOHN HUSSEY
Wife	SUSAN ENGEL
Juggler	ROBERT JENNINGS
Huckster	KEN WYNNE
Blae	PATSY BYRNE
A man looking for justice	TREVOR MARTIN
Eleanor	MAXINE AUDLEY
Henry	DEREK GODFREY
Becket	ALAN DOBIE
Cleric	DONALD LAYNE-SMITH
Gilbert Foliot	JOHN NETTLETON
Earl of Leicester	PAUL DAWKINS
Christ Church monks	KEN WYNNE JOHN HUSSEY
Young Henry, *the King's sons*	ROGER CROUCHER
Richard, *the King's sons*	DAVID BUCK
Geoffrey, *the King's sons*	IAN MCCULLOCH
John, *the King's sons*	MARTIN NORTON
Roger, *the King's son by Blae*	BRIAN SMITH
Messenger	SHAUN CURRY
Courtiers at Poitou	DARRYL KAVANN EDWARD ARGENT
Constance, *Geoffrey's wife*	SUSAN ENGEL
Margaret, *Young Henry's wife*	MARIAN DIAMOND
Captain	TREVOR MARTIN
Philip of France	PETER MCENERY
Old woman	MADOLINE THOMAS
Refugees	PAUL DAWKINS ROY MARSDEN CHERRY MORRIS IAN RICKETTS

Bishops: EDWARD ARGENT, TERENCE GREENIDGE, ROBERT JENNINGS, HENRY KNOWLES

Courtiers and Soldiers: MARGARETA BOURDIN, IMOGEN HASSALL, CAROLINE HUNT, CAROLINE MAUD, MARK MOSS, KENNETH RATCLIFFE, STUART RICHMAN, LESLIE SOUTHWICK

Directed by STUART BURGE

FOREWORD

HENRY PLANTAGENET was born in 1133, the son of Matilda (daughter of Henry I) and Geoffrey Plantagenet, Count of Anjou. During his boyhood England was suffering an eight-year-long agony of civil war, fought between his mother and Stephen of Blois. At the age of twenty-one he was King, and the wealthiest ruler in Europe. At fifty-six he was dead, the sword of State pawned, his heart broken. But 'he had laid the foundations of the English Common Law, upon which succeeding generations would build. Changes in the design would arise, but its main outlines would not be altered.'[1]

Between these two dates there is a seething cauldron of events, conflicts, purposes, errors, brilliance, human endurance, and human suffering, which could provide, in those thirty-five years, all that we need for a lifetime's study and contemplation of mankind. No single play could contain more than a splash from the brew. What to use and what to lose out of this feverish concentration of life? How far should fidelity to historical events be sacrificed to suit the theatre?

If a playwright is rash enough to treat real events at all, he has to accept a double responsibility: to drag out of the sea of detail a story simple enough to be understood by people who knew nothing about it before; and to do so without distorting the material he has chosen to use. Otherwise let him invent his characters, let him go to Ruritania for his history.

To try to re-create what has taken place in this world (or, indeed, to write about life at all) is to be faced by the task of putting a shape on almost limitless complexity. The necessity for the shaping—for 'making a play of it'—is inherent in us, because pattern and balance

[1] Winston Churchill, *The History of the English-speaking Peoples*, Vol. I.

are pervading facts of the universe. It is tempting to make a misleading simplification. In the absence of any other household-god, simplification becomes a gross superstition. It gives us the security of 'knowing', of being at home in events. We even call it reality, or getting down to the truth. But everything that we ignored remains to confute us.

I can't pretend that the play which follows has solved the problems, but consideration of them has dictated the way it should go. Though it follows chronology, it is not a chronicle play. The form it takes is one of memory and contemplation. The stage is William Marshal's mind, as though he were remembering the life of Henry; and the deviations from historical accuracy are on the whole no greater than might occur in a man's memory. The episodes are telescoped, but nothing in the play is entirely invented. Even the incident of the old woman and her feather-bed is on record.

But because, as far as I could, I have tried to do away with time and place, and to convey thirty years in one almost uninterrupted action, a few manipulations of fact have crept in. For instance, when Henry gives his age as twenty-nine, it is not the age he was at that precise point in the story (he was twenty-five), but the age he was two pages later, when he offers Canterbury to Becket. Then, also, he didn't die at Le Mans; he went on to make the desperate ride which he only plans in the play, and the meeting with Philip and Richard took place at Colombières. Nor did he die on the old woman's feather mattress, but on a bed at Chinon. The final episode, which I give to the townspeople of Le Mans, rightly belongs to Henry's own servants.

The character of Roger is a combination of two illegitimate sons, one born of a prostitute, and another who became Geoffrey the Chancellor. I renamed him to avoid the confusion of having two characters called Geoffrey.

The play has two themes: one a progression towards a portrait of Henry, a search for his reality, moving through versions of

'Where is the King?' to the unresolved close of 'He was dead when they came to him'. The other theme is Law, or rather the interplay of different laws: civil, canon, moral, aesthetic, and the laws of God; and how they belong and do not belong to each other.

It adds up to no more than a sketch of Henry. Just as the thirty-five years of his reign contain a concentration of the human condition, so his character covers a vast field of human nature. He was simple and royal (his nickname of 'Curtmantle' derived from the plain short cloak he wore), direct and paradoxical, compassionate and hard, a man of intellect, a man of action, God-fearing, superstitious, blasphemous, far-seeing, short-sighted, affectionate, lustful, patient, volcanic, humble, overriding. It is difficult to think of any facet of man which at some time he didn't demonstrate, except chastity and sloth.

My starting place was Mrs. J. R. Green's *Henry the Second.* Among the other books I read on the period, I am particularly indebted to Amy Kelly's *Eleanor of Aquitaine.*

C. F.

May 1961

NOTE TO THE SECOND EDITION

DURING the rehearsals for the English production I made a certain number of minor textual alterations, and added two short scenes: the conversation between the two monks about Becket's escape from England, and the scene between Henry, Roger, and Richard, before we come to Le Mans. This was a considerably condensed version of a scene which was played in the Dutch production.

After the performances at the Edinburgh Festival I made some more small changes, and reshaped those pages which extend from the news of the birth of Philip of France, to Richard's song after the coronation. I also rehandled the scene of Eleanor's court at Poitou.

I have begun both the Prologue and Act III with some words from Marshal, to establish him as the memory in which the action of the play takes place.

For the English production I reduced the length of the Prologue by half, but I have left it in its full form in the printed text. An audience hasn't a reader's privilege of being able to skip at will.

C. F.

1965

CHARACTERS

(in order of their appearance)

BARBER
WIFE
JUGGLER
HUCKSTER
BLAE
ANESTY
ELEANOR
WILLIAM MARSHAL
HENRY
BECKET
CLERIC
GILBERT FOLIOT
EARL OF LEICESTER
YOUNG HENRY, *the King's Son*
RICHARD }
GEOFFREY } *his brothers*
JOHN }
ROGER
MESSENGER
BECKET'S CROSS-BEARER
CONSTANCE, *Geoffrey's wife*
MARGARET, *Young Henry's wife*
CAPTAIN
PHILIP OF FRANCE
OLD WOMAN
FOUR REFUGEES
BISHOPS, MONKS, COURTIERS, SOLDIERS

PROLOGUE

BARBER

WIFE

JUGGLER

HUCKSTER

BLAE

ANESTY

ACT ONE

ELEANOR

WILLIAM MARSHAL

HENRY

BECKET

CLERIC

GILBERT FOLIOT

PROLOGUE

MARSHAL. Memory is not so harsh as the experience. Who can recall now the full devastation of the time when young Henry Plantagenet first came into his Kingdom? Henry Curtmantle, we sometimes called him, with his cloak as short as his need for sleep. His energy was like creation itself; he was giving form to England's chaos, an England that, after eight years of civil war, had no trade, no law, no conscience. Up and down the land he went, sparing neither himself nor us who were hauled along after him. Order was being born out of the sweat of those days and nights: a time of pugnacious reality, that still plays in my mind—beginning and ending, as it did in his thoughts also, with the people he governed.

On the edge of an improvised encampment. Cart shafts hung with clothes to make sleeping quarters. A wind is blowing. A man, a HUCKSTER, *is beating a drum. The King's* BARBER *and his* WIFE *shouting to each other above the wind and the drumming. Enter through the shadows a third man, a* JUGGLER.

BARBER. We're on the edge of the marsh. It's the noise of the frogs you can hear!

WIFE. What is it?

BARBER. The croaking of frogs!

JUGGLER. Men are getting rough where I've just come from.

BARBER. Who's beating the drum?

JUGGLER. Shine the lantern over here, will you? I've got blood coming out of me.

BARBER [*moving towards the* HUCKSTER]. Give us a chance to sleep, what's the matter with you?

HUCKSTER. I'm discouraging away the evils of the night.

BARBER. Discourage that drum for one.

JUGGLER. Bring us the light. The clumsy, excitable sons of bitches have dug a hole in me.

BARBER. What's the matter?

JUGGLER. They've gone mad up in front there, arguing over who has the best right to accommodation. I was trying to get past 'em, and got stuck on a knife. Hold the light still.

BARBER. Anyway, you won't die of it.

JUGGLER. The clumsy, excitable sons of bitches!

HUCKSTER. I'd be better off in London, I'll tell you that. If it rains on us now—*mercy domine*! You have to be like iron to follow the King.

JUGGLER. Whose bucket of water?

BLAE [*emerging from the dark*]. It's mine, dearie. Come on here; I'll cure you.

JUGGLER. I can manage, love.

WIFE. So she's learnt to cure 'em as well; very useful, I should think.

BLAE. I learn not to listen, see, Jack, I say nothing.

WIFE. If my husband was anything of a man, he would see I was sleeping somewhere better than this.

BARBER. She tells me a man would have elbowed his way up to the front and made himself known. 'I'm the King's barber', she says a man would have said, 'and you can all go and hook yourselves up on a bush'.

JUGGLER. I wouldn't be a man on those terms, Barber. Look what I got, and I was only walking past them.

WIFE. It sounds like they're slaughtering rats.

JUGGLER. It's plain vicious brawling. It doesn't hurt the King to change his mind where he's going to. No harm to him to land us up ten miles from no place; and no daylight, either, to see where to spit. And a dirty night coming up on the wind. He's lying well out of the weather in the farmhouse, with ten or twelve of the best of the lords lying alongside him. But when you've had that, there's an old splay-footed barn, and then you're down to the cow-house and the pigsties; and that's where the trouble started. Who's to have the accommodation? Who's to have the honour and precedence to lie down in the muck in the pigsty? That's the beginning of the argument, rising up to blaspheming oratory, then shouldering and shoving, and simple Jack has to go and pass them just when they fetch out their damned cutlery.

[*A yell is heard above the brawling.*

BARBER. There's somebody accommodated.

WIFE. We're better off where we are.

BARBER. That's what I said.

HUCKSTER. What sort of a world is it, Jesus hear me? You'd think when a man goes travelling with the King's Court he'd make a fortune for himself. But what's the outcome of it? Grinding forward, day after day, through miles of mud, and find your night's lodging in a filthy swamp.

BARBER. You can tell yourself it's a great benefit to the kingdom. That's the outcome of it. Law and order is the outcome. Haven't you got a memory for the smoke and ruin this land was? Mad, and murderous, and lawless, bleeding away like raw meat.

HUCKSTER. I can have more of that at home in my own bed.

JUGGLER. What's here? There's a light coming.

WIFE. See it? Yes, look, there it is.

BARBER. Who else is out in the night, looking for somewhere to sleep?

HUCKSTER. That's the marshes down there. That's not an ordinary light. That leads you off to sink over your ears in a mucky death. [*He nervously beats on the drum.*

BARBER. Give that a rest; give it up.

JUGGLER. Picking his way, the poor bloody man. We'll hollow at him.

BARBER. He's hollowing himself. [*To the* HUCKSTER.] Quiet, for God's sake!—Let's hear what he says.

[RICHARD ANESTY, *the traveller, calls from a short distance.*

ANESTY. Who's there to hear me?

JUGGLER. Any number.

ANESTY. Have I caught up with the King?

JUGGLER. You're on the verge of him. Struggle on.

BARBER. Who would come to this place looking for the King, where we don't know where we are ourselves?

WIFE. Where we wouldn't be if we knew better.

HUCKSTER. A hell of a valley to come and lodge in.

[*They wait for him. Enter* RICHARD ANESTY, *his sword drawn.*

JUGGLER. Draw into the circle, friend. We aren't quarrelsome.

ANESTY. God save you.

HUCKSTER. Let's hope so.

BARBER. You can save us your sword, as well.

JUGGLER. Put it by, man.

BARBER. If you think we're a lawless lot, no wonder, seeing us pitched out here in a black, spitting wind. But that's how the journey has gone, with the best of intentions. Otherwise we're decent men.

WIFE. He's the King's barber talking to you.

ANESTY. Then tell me where I can find the King.

JUGGLER. Show us your face.

ANESTY. Get me to the King.

BARBER. Steady, now, steady. What makes you think he'll see a gaunt, atrocious man rushing in on him out of the dark?

JUGGLER. Tell us your name.

ANESTY. Richard Anesty.

BARBER. What do you want with the King, Richard Anesty?

ANESTY. Simply a matter of birthright: of common justice. Where shall I find him?

BARBER. Wait, now, wait! Give us a proper explanation of yourself.

ANESTY. To satisfy the barber? So that's what I've come to. Well, the name is Anesty. My property was a fair property: was heft off me in the civil wars. It's taken five years, going through the courts, trying to get it back again. I'm sick of that particular labyrinth; it breaks the spirit. The King's the only answer. He'll see the matter set right: loves the law, hates the grabbing barony. He'll see the future gives me a world of my proper rights. Which way do I go to him?

BARBER. No way, at this hour of the night.

ANESTY. Who do you think will stop me now?

BARBER. You stay here, sir, as I say to you.

ANESTY. Not for a barber!

BARBER [*holding his arm*]. Then we'll have to keep you, for your own good!

JUGGLER [*taking the other;* ANESTY *struggles*]. Calm your soul, sir.

ANESTY. Right, when I've seen the King.

BARBER. And that's first thing in the morning. He's seeing all the men then who have a reasonable cause for complaining, before we move off.

BLAE. At six o'clock.

WIFE. You can believe her. She gets the accurate information always, one way and another.

ANESTY. But I'm within yards of putting my hand to him. Do you know what you're asking?

JUGGLER. Well, the time will pass easy enough if you're sleeping.

ANESTY. I've been searching for him seven weeks and two days. I've had two horses die on the road, the last an hour or so ago, three miles short of catching up with you. There was no way of knowing, from one day to the next, where the King would be.

BARBER. Right, sir. That's his whole plan and purpose. Find out the true state of the courts of law and the administration of his kingdom, is what he is after; so come up on them unawares is what he does. Thursday at Nottingham, says the itinerary. So the judges at Nottingham keep sober Monday, Tuesday, Wednesday, put off accepting any bribes till Friday, rub the dirt off their hands, and sit down to business as punctual as the light. And where is the King's majesty? The King's majesty is in Sheffield.

ANESTY. I know it very well.

JUGGLER. Well, here you are; get some sleep. The morning's not so far off. You'll have no trouble from the King if you've got a good claim.

HUCKSTER. Though you might wonder, looking at us here. He'll march us all to death to get his law and order, though I'll say this, he's sorry for you when you're dead. Concerning the foreign sailors wrecked on our coast, per example, and the killing, robbing, and stripping thereof, he wept like a sweating cistern, as we saw at Whitstable. The veins in his head stood up the size of ropes, condemning the practices to perjury-come. So we know to be butchered if we want to be well thought of.

BARBER [*indicating the* HUCKSTER *with his head*]. A highly nervous trading kind of man, with no wide thoughts at all for the world's good.—Haven't you got a memory for the smoke and ruin this land was? Mad, and murderous, and lawless, bleeding away like raw meat!

JUGGLER. Half a lifetime of it, if you can put that out of your memory.

BARBER. Foul injustice done to good men. As this good man here himself has suffered, so he tells us.

JUGGLER. This good man here is fast asleep.

BARBER. There it is, you see: good men can sleep now, under the wisdom of King Henry.

WIFE. Under a cart, if you wouldn't mind noticing.

BARBER. The wind is taking the clouds off. There it is: times are improving.

HUCKSTER. But I'm not, Jesus hear me.

JUGGLER. Six good hours insensible. I'll enjoy that. Goodnight, friends.

[*The camp settles down to sleep. A horn begins to blow, coming nearer; shouts and a growing murmur.*

JUGGLER [*groaning*]. What's the trouble now?

HUCKSTER. Isn't there to be any night between days in this King's world, for God's sake?

BARBER. We'd better find out.

VOICE [*coming nearer*]. Break up camp, get on the road!

HUCKSTER. They've gone out of their minds.

VOICE. Break up camp!

WIFE. What do they mean? Now? In the night?

VOICE. The King's in the saddle! Hurry yourselves! We're making for Kettering!

JUGGLER. What fool drunk has started this?

BARBER [*returning from inquiry*]. The camp's breaking up. We've got to move.

WIFE. Kettering!

JUGGLER. That means the best part of twenty miles before morning.

HUCKSTER. If a man can't have his lawful sleep, to hell with the law.

[*The camp is busy and noisy, the lanterns moving, the carts being wheeled away.*

BARBER [*shaking* ANESTY *as he passes him*]. Better wake up, Richard Anesty. The King has left for Kettering.

ANESTY. The King—

BARBER. The King is riding off to Kettering.

ANESTY [*struggling to his feet*]. No, no, no! It isn't light yet. You swore to me you would bring me to him in the morning.

BARBER. So we thought we would, but we're moving on.

ANESTY. You don't know what you're saying! I have to see him! He has only got to lean a moment from his saddle! What can I do? How can I go on?—Where is the King?

[*The stage empties and darkens.*

Where shall I find the King? A law that's just and merciful! Do I have to walk on for ever, looking for that?

[*He trudges after the receding noise of the wagons.*

Where is the King?

[*The wind blows in the dark, drops to a calm, and gradually the light increases on an empty hall in Westminster, no person there except the Queen*, ELEANOR, *standing alone.*

END OF PROLOGUE

ACT ONE · 1158–63

Westminster. ELEANOR. *Enter* WILLIAM MARSHAL, *grinning.*

MARSHAL. The King's arrived in the yard, ma'am, with the Chancellor.

ELEANOR. And every man in London appears to be smiling.
What is it, Marshal? Every man
Who has come in out of the street is either grinning,
Or sprawling a great hand across his mouth,
As though there were something of obscene pleasure in the world outside.

MARSHAL. Well, possibly it might be a general feeling of success. As far as we can gather, the Chancellor has come back from France with what he wanted. That's one cause for smiling. When you think of the state of grievance the French have been in, ever since you divorced their King and rode off with your own property—that's a second cause for smiling. *Où se sont évanouis le Poitou et l'Aquitaine?*

ELEANOR. Marshal, you've gone out of your mind.

MARSHAL. You must admit, ma'am, that was a pretty damned effective joke. When you think of them seeing the Kingdom of France reduced by a half, on one Palm Sunday afternoon.

ELEANOR. You expect me to believe that this grin on your face has been there for eleven years? Now tell me the truth. What is the joke? Are the filthy actors out in the yard?

MARSHAL. No, ma'am. It's the King and the Chancellor.

ELEANOR. Being witty enough to make all men smile. Or was it horse-play?

MARSHAL. Both, ma'am.

ELEANOR. This island can never have been better entertained.

MARSHAL. There they were, the King and the Chancellor,
Riding together along Cheapside, the crown
And the croney, in great pleasure together.
There was a fairly disgusting beggar-man,
Best part naked, lifting up one of his crutches
Across the King's path. 'Poor lousy fellow',
The King said, reining in his horse.—'Dear lord of justice',
Said the beggar. He knew his onions; he understood
Just how to come at the King's generosity.
He said he was born at Le Mans, the same as the King.
Everybody knows what affection the King has
For his own birthplace. And then a hard-up story
That jerked a quick tear out of the King. 'Christ,'
He said, 'we'll have no naked men. Christ's
Charity, Thomas, let him have your cloak!'
'Give him yours, Henry,' Becket said:
'This is *your* deed of grace.' 'It 's too old, and too short',
Said the King. 'It would be no charity to his arse.'
And he made a grab at the Chancellor's cloak—cinnamon
Velvet, a new one—and they wrestled on horseback, to take it
And keep it, until every man round was laughing himself
To water, and the Chancellor gave in.
So the King threw down the cloak, obliterating
The beggar, and we all rode forward happy.

ELEANOR. A deed of grace, gracefully done,
And very delicately reported. Here is the King.

[WILLIAM MARSHAL *withdraws. Enter* HENRY, *chuckling, and* BECKET.

HENRY. His dignity shaken, but thanks to me
There 's much joy in heaven over his charity.

BECKET. Ma'am, you will have to excuse a naked Chancellor.

ELEANOR. As God made you, Becket. I've no objection.

HENRY. Embrace him, Eleanor. He has worked his charms
On Paris.

ELEANOR. I heard so. It's a happy thing
That he lives in this modern world, to give us his company.

BECKET. There would be no Becket, without the King.
Nor, I might add, much sign of the King's magnificence
Without his Chancellor. I shall be ruined, Henry,
Trying to keep up your personal splendour for you,
To match the importance of your position!

HENRY. You love it.

BECKET. It's just as well I love it. It impressed Louis.

ELEANOR. Poor Louis with his endless daughters.
It would rather seem, if he is letting us marry
Our young Henry to the baby Margaret,
He despairs at last of having a son. The skies
Are curiously empty for Louis, his long prayers
Are ineffectual.

BECKET. Completely so.
And his disappointed Majesty of France
Has come to an agreement with us over the question
Of his daughter's dowry. He is willing—at least,
I'll say he is prepared, when the children marry
To make over to his daughter the country of the Vexin.

ELEANOR. With all its castles. Of course, Becket.
It was what you went for.

HENRY. So you can chew
On that, Becket. No commendation from Eleanor.
She learned her behaviour from an oracle;

What she expects, is what occurs. And what
You went for, we have got. And what we have got
Is natural, because it was necessary.
And that puts us clearly into the ascendent
For a term of good order, while we do our work.
From the Arctic circle to the Pyrenees
The King's peace is holding secure.

BECKET. And God's peace, too, no doubt.

HENRY. No doubt.
It wouldn't surprise me.
Not a son is born to Louis, though he would give
God his place in his bed if he could get one.
But four good boys to me.
There's God articulate, if ever a god spoke.
Four strong Plantagenet males born
To a kingdom worthy of God's admiration.

ELEANOR. All being well.

HENRY. What isn't well already
Is getting down on to its knees to be cured.
God's light, there's no anarchy to come worse
Than I've already transformed into good government,
Unless they drive me to a harrowing of hell.

ELEANOR. Or unless you drive them back to anarchy
To be free of your endless tramping up and down.
I never see a man in the Court who hasn't a limp,
The soles of his feet as raw with blisters
As yours are, Henry. For the Queen's peace,
Will you sit down?

HENRY. Why not? I should like to know if there's anything
Our dear friend here of the ten talents
Can fail at. Put him in command of the field,

You can see the horse under him grow two hands taller
While Becket stacks the countryside with Christian
Corpses. Eh, Tom? And has to be restrained.
Ship him to the continent as Chancellor
To work a delicate diplomacy,
He treats the road to Paris to such an immense
Procession of the mad world, and all singing in dialect:
Hawks, and dogs; and longtailed apes
Up on the backs of the horses: all his gold plate
And his private chapel, a holy menagerie
Of opulence and power—
Every mouth in France drops too wide open
To shut again in time to deny us
Anything we came to ask.
But then you see him here, dispensing charity,
There's the deacon in him. What are you, Becket?
Force, craft, or the holy apprentice?

BECKET. The King's representative. And full of faults.
I do what I can.

HENRY. But you're not the whole of a man's capability,
Thomas, for all your talents: I know you to be
An incorruptible virgin: your virginity's
As crass extravagant as the rest of your ways of living.
If every man gave up women in God's name,
Where in God's name would be the men
To give up women in a generation's time?
I tell you, Becket, for the sake of divine worship
You'd better apply the flesh.

BECKET. I am content,
Henry, to be one man, and not the human race.

ELEANOR. It's as well that there should be someone in this country
To undertake chastity for the King.

HENRY [*a pause*]. Well, there you have your permission.
Fill the office of my virginity
And scrape a living out of it if you can.

BECKET. Perfectly willing.

HENRY. I shall expect a sainthood
When my term of the world is over. Put it to the Pope.
[*He has shuffled over some documents.*
Have you seen this, Becket? These crozier-clutching monkeys,
Ramming home their shutters against the common
Light of day: but the day comes, despite 'em!

BECKET. What is it?

HENRY [*throwing a parchment at him*]. There it is.

ELEANOR. Clearly the findings of an ecclesiastical court.

BECKET [*reading*]. The case of the Canon of Lincoln.

HENRY. The reverend Canon of rape and murder, who thinks
Because they shaved his head in a holy circle
He can grow the hair of an ape on his breast and his genitals.
He thinks he has the divine right
To cut throats and not hang for it.

BECKET. The Bishop
Could find no proof of his guilt. That was why he was acquitted.

HENRY. They can reverse the acquittal. The Sheriff
Has sworn the man is guilty. They can pass him over
To the secular arm, where a man is known by his crimes
And not by his credentials. God's seat,
I mean to make a fair and governable England;
One justice, not two. The Church will soon
Turn every criminal into a priest, to avoid the gallows;
And the other honest, poor damned sons of Cain
Who get slewed into crime in a five-minute passion
Are hanged by the neck.

BECKET. All right, Henry.
Let's leave the poor damned sons of Cain to God, then.

ELEANOR. At least for this afternoon. We met here
To welcome Becket. As I am neither a Bishop
Nor a raping Canon
It's no argument which need detain me.

HENRY. I've heard no argument. Tom loves the law,
And he knows as well as I do the day is soon coming
When those who deviate will be compelled
Into the common pattern. There it is:
Patience restored. Sit down. I'll tell you
What my memory is celebrating today.
Not only Becket's triumphant return.
What else makes this a feast of the Angevin succession?

ELEANOR. What day is it?

HENRY. Unhorsed at the first shock.

ELEANOR. What day of the month?

BECKET. The sixteenth of September.
I can think of nothing: no battle, no marriage, no birth,
No death, no treaty, of which the anniversary
Falls on the sixteenth of September.

ELEANOR. I remember
Very well. It was the day, eleven years ago,
When I first met him; or, to be accurate,
The day I suffered his invasion:
For I can tell you, Becket,
He came forward to kiss my hand
Like a man who has just broken down the door.
I'm not at all certain he didn't ride in
Through the doorway on a horse.

HENRY. Becket, I swear
I sidled in like an egg-bound goose,
I held her in such tremendous awe, this woman
Who had been the inspiration of poets
Ever since I could understand language,
And the haunter of male imagination
Ever since I could understand sex.

ELEANOR. You hear him
Working at his arithmetic, Becket,
And grubbing up his advantage of years.

BECKET. Time walks by your side, ma'am, unwilling to pass.
But Henry lives and does his work
In a race of nights and days which are piling the years
Up on him fast.

HENRY. Twenty-nine, you methusalem!
I can live to bury you twice over. God knows
Time isn't a fellow workman to be trusted
In any great patient endeavour. It's never
Far from my mind. So much the more
The men who impede me had better take care.

ELEANOR. We were beginning to tame him. Now he's off
Trying to walk time to a standstill. Come back to the past,
Henry—eleven years ago today—

HENRY. By God, I went to her cap in hand,
Heart in mouth, and by God she was everything
Reported of her.

BECKET. And more, Henry.

ELEANOR. No, no;
I protest at that. Less, as God will judge me,
I was less than reported. My reputation
Wasn't spared in the French court then. And, to cap all,

As a variation of boredom, I gave to Louis
Another disastrous daughter. A waste of labour.
And the Abbot of Clairvaux—
After praying, I hope, for the accurate word—
Called me the evil genius of France.
That was at least something to be
In that miserable autumn, but not
My entire ambition. And, more or less then,
The door was torn off its hinges by the Duke of Normandy.
Henry was standing there eyeing me, ready
To start creating the world.

HENRY. And not by accident,
This meeting with her. It was in the great
Pattern of events. Old Merlin predicted it.

BECKET. Stuff and nonsense.

HENRY. That's your opinion.

BECKET. Well, I can think of better springs of action
Than a popular forgery.

HENRY. Not the cause: I never said so:
But a welcome confirmation.

ELEANOR. You see how easily a woman is fooled, Becket.
In the tender fancy of my heart I thought
He was marrying me for my great possessions.
But you see I was only a superstition.
He took me, as he would take the salt he spilled,
And threw me over his shoulder to improve his luck.

HENRY. The Queen is angling for a quarrel, Becket,
Because she knows she is looking as ageless
As the Sea of Marmara, and no one has said so.

BECKET. I have said so.

HENRY. Then say it again;
She likes to hear you.

ELEANOR. Being the wife of Louis
Was like being married to a priest; with Henry
It is like being married to a jobbing Jupiter.
Tell me, how was Louis when you saw him, Becket?

BECKET. Courteous, ma'am, and over anxious.

ELEANOR. Unchanged. Frayed to ribbons whether to be
A king or an archbishop. It was always so.
He could never co-ordinate the two worlds.

BECKET. It was charming to see him
Pressing back against the wall at the sight
Of the least little monk, to let him take precedence,
Though the little monk drowned himself in blushes
And would have given his life
To have been allowed to bow himself out backwards.
But the King went on murmuring, 'No, no, dear and beloved
Brother in Christ Jesus, after you, if you please;
My kingdom is nothing to the kingdom of heaven;
You have the superiority; I must insist!'

HENRY. Excellent, I can hear him! You're any man
You want to be, Becket, I told you! Let's hear him again!

ELEANOR. As in Passion week eleven years ago.

HENRY. Louis, divorce your wife; excuse me,
I have a use for her.

ELEANOR. Your evil spirit
Is prepared to leave you, Louis.

BECKET [*in the voice of Louis*]. Then may heaven
Help me with grace to suffer your going,
Amen; and France, taking the lower place,

Be first in God's mercy, and bear all things patiently
In the service of heaven.

HENRY. Amen, amen.

ELEANOR. Am I free, Louis?

BECKET [*in the voice of Louis*].
If to St. Peter's chair and in the will of God
We are not one, by my obedience we are two.

ELEANOR. Redemption by divine arithmetic!

[*They break into laughter.*

HENRY. Which reminds me, Tom: I'm giving you Canterbury.
By your own merit, Archbishop as well as Chancellor.

[*A silence.* BECKET *stands frozen.*

HENRY. Well, you immeasurable man. Your air
Of astonished innocence doesn't convince me. Don't
Pretend you never considered the chance of this
In one of your forward-looking silences
As soon as you knew that Theobald was dead?

BECKET. This is what Louis tried to do:
Insisting on his Chancellor for a bishopric
Against the nomination of the Chapter.
And you know what came of it. The Pope intervened
With anathema, and Louis had to give in.

HENRY. Louis can only get daughters, and I get sons,
Even on the same wife. What's the argument?

BECKET. There's one man in particular, Foliot of London,
And six or seven others besides, who by
Their learning, integrity, piety, loyalty
And cast of mind, are a better choice for Canterbury.

HENRY. And who is a better choice for England?

BECKET. Any mere minor canon or choirmaster
Living as intently to his church
As a workman who bows his head
Over his chosen craft.

HENRY. And who
Is a better choice for me?

BECKET. I am not.
Ask any hundred random men,
They'll tell you so. The Church itself
Neither waits for me, nor wants me; rather
Deplores me than otherwise. And I'm not a man
Whose confidence thrives on its own. What I do well
I do because men believe I will do it well
Before ever the thing is begun. The fruit
On the tree forms larger in a willing climate,
Or anyway I found it so in my own
Experience. I care for men's opinion.
I doubt if I should ever be
Sufficient in myself, to hold my course
Without any approval. No one would say
I was made of the stuff of martyrs. So if you ever
Trusted to my perception—

HENRY. Never,
My friend. I trust your administration,
Grasp of the law, charm of persuasion,
And your like-thinking with my own thought—

BECKET. Natural in a Chancellor.

HENRY. And natural
In my long-tried friend, Tom Becket.

BECKET. But what is natural in an Archbishop?

HENRY. Precisely what is natural in Tom Becket.
Your election is simple. To the majority
Of men, inevitable.

BECKET. One thing is simple.
Whoever is made Archbishop will very soon
Offend either you, Henry, or his God.
I'll tell you why. There is a true and living
Dialectic between the Church and the state
Which has to be argued for ever in good part.
It can't be broken off or turned
Into a clear issue to be lost or won.
It 's the nature of man that argues;
The deep roots of disputation
Which dug in the dust, and formed Adam's body.
So it's very unlikely, because your friend
Becomes Primate of England, the argument will end.
As Chancellor, my whole mind could speak for yours,
Because I knew the Church had for her tongue
A scholar and a saintly man who was not to be
Brow-beaten. But now Theobald is dead.
The English Church has lost its tongue. Do you mean
That I should now become that tongue,
To be used in argument between you and me?
Because, if so, we shall not be as we have been.

HENRY. You will miss your falcons, of course, if you decide
That blood sports are too secular.
But which of us is going to change his nature
Or his understanding? Together we have understood
The claims men have on us
And how to meet them. Whatever your office
This truth is unalterable, the truth being one.

BECKET. The truth, like all of us, being of many dimensions,

And men so placed, they stake their lives on the shape of it
Until by a shift of their position, the shape
Of truth has changed.

ELEANOR. Hardly a conclusion, I fancy,
Which the good scholar and saintly man who trained you
Would have applauded with both hands. Nevertheless
Consider it, Henry. Conserve the blessings
You have already.

HENRY. The blessings I have already
Are there to be blessed with.
And the future is waiting to be blessed by us,
In spite of the men who drag their feet. I can see
He means to refuse.

BECKET. I haven't said so.

HENRY. I can see he means to.

BECKET. I haven't said so.
But listen to the things I fear. However much
We both imperatively want it otherwise,
You're dividing us, and, what is more, forcing
Yourself and me, indeed the whole kingdom,
Into a kind of intrusion on the human mystery,
Where we may not know what it is we're doing,
What powers we are serving, or what is being made of us.
Or even understand the conclusion when it comes.
Delivering us up, in fact, to universal workings
Which neither you nor I wish to comply with
Or even to contemplate. If this should be so,
Do you still propose that I should accept Canterbury?

ELEANOR. Well, which is it to be, Henry, to predict
The future, Becket or Merlin?

HENRY. Now he's master of excuses.
Too complacent, is he, to enlarge himself
To the size of the new world we have under our hand?
But foresee this, then: if King and Archbishop
Can work in affection, the Church will be content
And calm. If not: waste of hours, energy,
Opportunity; and much loss
And peril to souls will come of it; and, worse,
Loss of the time we need, to give England
An incorruptible scaffolding of law
To last her longer than her cliffs.

BECKET. You remember
When the Archbishop was dying, he sent for me
And I didn't go. Now, on your own insistence,
I see I do go after all, though now
Too late to have any happiness in going.
According to your will, then, Henry.

HENRY. All right, you confer the favour. I thought that I did.
But what difference? We shall go ahead.
Make away with your uncertainties, man.
Anything unaccustomed has a doubtful look
Till it grows to be a part of our thinking.
Why shouldn't you keep your falcons?
God will expect something of the kind
From an Archbishop who was born in England.
We'll make up to Him for it by establishing
Order, protection, and justice
For the man who has a shirt or the man who has not.
A pity the whole of the earth is not to be
Serene in our keeping. But there are still
The four good Plantagenet males to come.
We must leave them something to do.

Come and see that nest of young eagles, Tom.
You can describe to Harry the good points
Of Margaret of France, if you think you can make
An infant sound like a desirable wife.

ELEANOR. You've drawn blood from Becket, Henry.
The city sunshine, and the new English archbishop
Are equally cold and pale.
And besides, he has made a long journey for you.
You should give him time to rest.

BECKET. The sea was rough.

HENRY. Do as you like, Tom. Be your own man
Until tomorrow. [*Exit* HENRY.

ELEANOR. And, ever after, be his
In every particular. The free and fallen
Spirits we may think we are,
You and I and the nest of young eagles,
Have our future state only in a world of Henry.
I should go and get your rest, Becket, before
You are led away into captivity by this new well-ordered world.

[*She follows* HENRY. BECKET *stands unmoving.* WILLIAM MARSHAL *comes forward with a cloak.*

MARSHAL. They've brought over another cloak for you from the Chancery, my lord Chancellor.—Will you wear it, my lord?—They brought it to replace the one you parted with.—This is your own, from the Chancery, sir.

[*He puts the cloak on to* BECKET'*s shoulders.*

BECKET. Is the day much colder?

MARSHAL. I don't think so. But, if you remember, you gave away your cloak—

BECKET. Tell me, Marshal, do you know yourself, who you are?

MARSHAL. I daresay I could pick myself out among two or three men, if I took thought.

BECKET. You have the best of it.—Take good care of the King.

MARSHAL. Why not? And the King can take good care of us. But what's your thought there, sir?

[BECKET *moves on out of sight.*

Why urge that on me?—[*He turns to the audience.*] I was soon to know. What was one had become two. The simple and reasonable action, at the very moment it came to life, was neither simple nor limited to reason. There it is. The logic of events has never been argued in the schools, as far as I know. There was the morning full of life, like an unbroken colt; but the moment the King, with a good will and strong knees, got astride it, God only knows what whistle it was answering; but it made history, whatever that is.—The day when Becket was consecrated Archbishop was a bright, fresh day; what clouds there were were easy-moving; and, except for a sharp indrawing of breath from the Chapter at Canterbury, we were all in the humour of progress, the rich men inside the cathedral, wary over their privileges, or the poor men outside, concerned with hope, all for the moment willing to presume a benefit from this move the King had made: firm, reasonable, new for those who looked for change, not too new for those who prospered in stability, and therefore promising, making for unity. The whole significance of unity was not debated, nor what fires can forge a diverse multitude into one mind. But for the present, at any rate. . . . Excuse me. [*He peers into the shadows.*] Come here.

[BLAE *comes forward.*

Who let you through?

BLAE. Nobody let me through. He was dead against it. I didn't need any youngster like that to tell me to stand and be recognized. I know who I am as well as he does. What I've come for is no business of his.

MARSHAL. This is no such free world, sweetheart. Come on, I'll see you safely outside again.

BLAE. I wouldn't put you to the trouble.—Keep your hands for your food.

MARSHAL. The boys all know where to find you, don't worry. If business is so bad, coming here isn't going to change it.

BLAE. Change isn't what I came for. I want something taken care of.

MARSHAL. I'll take care of you, for a good start. You can follow the Court when it's out on the road, but when we are back to London you stay home.

BLAE. So I do. But there's something I have to say to the King.

MARSHAL. You're not going to see the King.

BLAE. I don't have to; I can tell who he is in the dark.

MARSHAL. So that's what you're up to. Then let me say this to you, if you haven't got sense enough to know it; there's a private world, and a public world, there's a world of night, and a world of day, and if you dare to get one confused with the other I'll break my heart for the way you'll end up. The sooner I get you out of here, the better it will be for you.

BLAE. The King will see no harm comes to me, I can tell you that now.

MARSHAL. The King isn't going to have the chance.

[*He throws her over his shoulder.*

BLAE. He won't have you do this, not to the mother of a son of his.

[MARSHAL *stops and puts her down.* HENRY *stands upstage, unseen by them.*

MARSHAL. That's a pretty presentable story. Born with a label tied to his ear, *filius Henrici*, with a birth-mark of the Plantagenet leopard stamped sheer across him.

BLAE. You might have seen him. How did you know?

MARSHAL. Because otherwise you'd be out of your mind to risk laying charges against the King for the sake of what you can get out of it. I can tell you now what you'll get out of it—

HENRY. How do you know he's a boy of mine?

BLAE. It's him!

MARSHAL [*aside to her*]. Now will you run?

BLAE [*under her breath*]. I'm not doing wrong.

HENRY. How do you know he's a boy of mine?

BLAE. He says it himself, sir, in every pug look he gives me.

HENRY. What do you want?

BLAE. To know what's to be done with him. That's all, sir. What's to be done with you, I say to him, playing about with half the muck of your father's kingdom on your face and your knees?

HENRY. Go and take a look at him, Marshal. If he looks like mine, bring him to me. If he looks like mine to me, Becket can raise him and train him at the Chancery.

BLAE. Sir, you're a good King, a good man to all of us.

HENRY. Go and lick him clean, and give my face a chance to shine through him. And don't expect anything more from it.

BLAE. Nothing on earth, you can have my word. Myself is myself, sir, and that I can make do to look after. I give you my word—

HENRY. All right; exist unexplained. Get home.

BLAE. Yes, sir, my lord. [*Exit* BLAE.

HENRY. You see what comes, Marshal, of a wet summer.
That August at Hereford, the rain came down on us
Like a high sea slapping over a cockle boat

For six days, remember?
A week of good life wasted in a flood.

[*A* CLERIC *has entered with a letter.*

What's this?

CLERIC. From his Grace of Canterbury, my lord.
He sends you his love and obedience.

HENRY. Two words, love and obedience. What
Does he expect me to do with them, when I never see him?
Haven't I given him time enough yet
To get used to being cock of the cloistral walk?
There's a child in him; he loves himself
In a new frock. That's it, Marshal, you fetch
That sprig of Plantagenet the whore has got,
And we'll make him as good a Chancellor in twenty years.
We'll see what life comes out of that churn-up
Of rain and Hereford mud and boredom and semen
And prostitution. Go and fetch him.

MARSHAL. I'll take a look, my lord, and try and judge what I find there.

[*Exit* MARSHAL. HENRY, *who has broken open the letter, reads it.*

HENRY. Did he tell you to say his love and obedience?

CLERIC. Yes, my lord.

HENRY. Then he told you a lie.

CLERIC. My lord?

HENRY. He made you bring me a damned lie! Watch out, you pious little fellow, how much of your heart you give to faith. We've hanged God once, to fulfil the scriptures. So now tell me what reason God still has to keep the strain of treachery so active in us. Eh? You tell me that.

CLERIC. Oh, my lord, watch your words.

HENRY. What kind of a farce is good faith and loyalty?

ELEANOR [*standing upstage*]. You tell me that.

HENRY [*looking at her*]. I am hurt by the child in this Tom Becket.

[*Enter* GILBERT FOLIOT, *Bishop of London, the King's confessor.*

ELEANOR. What has he done?

HENRY. Resigned from the Chancellorship, with his love and obedience. Come here, Foliot. You'd better absolve me of a blasphemy, or something of the sort. It upset our holy innocent, here.

FOLIOT. Are you truly penitent?

HENRY. Yes, yes, yes, come on!

[FOLIOT *begins to speak in Latin, the words of absolution, and then breaks off.*

FOLIOT. *Ego te absolvo*—My lord, will you give me your attention?

HENRY [*still reading Becket's letter*]. God in a suicide's grave! Will you listen to this? . . . 'Not wishing now to be in the royal court . . . diddle, diddle, diddle . . . to have leisure for prayers, and to superintend the business of the Church . . .'—Who put him there to pray? There are ten thousand monks, with nothing else to do except say his prayers for him.

[FOLIOT *concludes the absolution, fairly hurriedly:*

FOLIOT. *—in nomine patris et filii et spiritu sancti.*

HENRY. Amen.—Christ in glory, what's been the truth of him over these years? The whole motive and labour of his mind, as he showed it to us, was the wise conduct of this poor, tormented kingdom. And he made a fortune out of it, which I didn't grudge him. But, by God, that was all he cared for, to be the unsurpassable Becket, and nothing at all for the shaping of a just world: his mouth was making words at me, like a purse farting.

ELEANOR. Now he will see your justice demonstrated,
This angelic justice,
Hearing all voices, and weighing them in its heart,
Having no person or desires. Show us, Henry.

HENRY. Where is he, then? Ever since his consecration
He has turned his back on us, crouching down in Canterbury
As though he had conquered a rock, stuck his cross on it,
And meant to keep a sulking stretch of water
Between him and me.

CLERIC. Sir, speaking of what we see at Canterbury, you would praise, as we do, how the finger of God has touched him; how utterly he has put aside all ostentation; how he feasts the poor, visits the sick, and every day washes the feet of thirteen beggars.

HENRY. A very sagacious and elaborate performance. I hope the beggars are paid for it.

FOLIOT. We must remember, my lord, the difficulties for him are very great. An immense talent, as we know; but, even so, even you, my lord, must have expected an uncertain period of readjustment. He is anxious to please. It will be interesting to see how he achieves what you have set him to do.

HENRY. We know you will be interested. So does he. The devil of an interest.

FOLIOT. False. I had no ambition to be in his place, though I believe it was said.

HENRY. It was said so, I believe. But you deny it. Love and obedience have been said. But here it's denied. When do we have the truth?

Enter BECKET

ELEANOR. Ask him. [HENRY *turns his head away.*
He has left his rock.

HENRY. What am I supposed to make of this?

BECKET. What is natural because it is necessary.
I am one man, not two. My heart and reason
Both give me the same answer.

HENRY. I can see no heart.
What reason?

BECKET. You gave me spiritual charge of the kingdom.
I take it, then, the kingdom's need
Is that I should carry this charge in good earnest.

HENRY. The kingdom, not a country parish. You know
Very well the need of the kingdom you serve.
It's a living land, not a charge of kneeling peasants
Obedient to a bell. And you know the Church
That you're the head of, with its delight in substance
Growing on itself like sin. Power and privilege,
The swollen spiritual legs we have to stand on!
I'll tell you, Becket, why it is you have drained
All the warmth out of yourself down there in Canterbury.
Because the King's truth is the truth you still believe.
You kept clear of me to give yourself
A spiritual authority you know you're weak in.
What's your answer to that?

BECKET. If it is true
That I'm weak in spiritual authority—it isn't
For me to deny it—should you not thank God
That I mean to gain it? What is the worth of a kingdom
If the head of its Church has no spiritual authority?

HENRY. What is the worth of spiritual authority
If the lives under it are lived in anarchy?

BECKET. What have I done that proposes anarchy?

HENRY. Contradictory power is what you propose.
There is hardly one thing I have reached out for
In these last months, which hasn't been obstructed
From Canterbury. But I see you, Becket:
You mean the Church to be answerable for nothing
Except itself, and yourself to be answerable
Only to the old would-be infallible Italian
Who rattles his keys of heaven and hell whichever
Way expedience turns him.

FOLIOT. *Te absolvo.* My lord,
Whatever the provocation, there's no advantage
In turning your scorn on the Holy Father.

HENRY. Is there not? Then I'm taking no advantage.

BECKET. Henry, one of us there has to be
To whom the single care is not of this world.

HENRY. Very well; give up this world.
Contend against me like an opposite.
See that the spiritual power is powerful in the spirit.
Indeed, go on, be smitten with a great light
And relieve us all of a load of darkness.
Show us, my friend—we are hungry to see it—
The humility, the patience, and the poverty,
The movement into grace, the entire surrender
And sacrifice of the self.
And not by a demonstration of foot-washing.

BECKET. Why suddenly talk like a woman,
Contriving an argument when you know the answers?
You, Henry, of all men, who cry out
For a demonstration of order, for a house of men
So lucid and strong it will never be confounded.
See the Church likewise. If she should have

No definition in terms of the world, no shepherd
To guard her rule and substance, she would soon be thrust
Into any corner that man, trampling forward
Towards his places of possession,
Thought fit to leave open. What is not seen or heard
But yet endures has to be shown and spoken.
How, then, without rich form of ritual
And ceremony, shall we convey
The majesty of eternal government,
Or give a shape to the mystery revealed
Yet as a mystery?

HENRY. All right, perform the mystery, demonstrate
The mysterious order: baptize us, reprove us,
Absolve us, and bury us; but in so far
As your body sweats like the rest of us,
You owe me obedience.

BECKET. And in so far
As you live, Henry, like the rest of us
In a universe of powers outside your government:
And in so far
As everything beyond the immediate moment
Ends in speculation: and in so far
As not even the predictions of Merlin
Can provide us with a living geometry
Of what we do, or what's done to us, in these
Things you owe your obedience to the Church.

HENRY. I owe no obedience to a man who cheats my trust in him.
None at all to an ostentatious humbug
Who dragged himself up by the shoulders of the kingdom
And once up, kicked it away. Your breeding
Wasn't prepared for the full extent of your talents,
Not to serve this world, or God either.

BECKET. You have borne with me pretty well. I must live in hope
That God's patience won't fall far short of yours, my lord.
—Your permission to withdraw.

HENRY. In a fury, good;
You're still living, then; there's a warmth
Residing somewhere in this reverend cadaver.

BECKET. I will go apart for a time.

HENRY. Do, for a time,
And scour yourself with an hour of good thinking.
Return Tom Becket, a man unwilling to deceive
Either himself or me.

[BECKET *turns as though to speak again.* FOLIOT *touches his arm.*

FOLIOT. Apart, apart. You are not ready to speak. This need never have happened. Come away.

[BECKET *moves away,* FOLIOT *and the* CLERIC *with him.* HENRY *turns aside to* WILLIAM MARSHAL, *who has returned.*

HENRY. Well, what's the answer?

MARSHAL. I saw the boy. He struck at me with a fist the size of an acorn and told me I was an old what I am not, my lord.

HENRY. Would you say he is mine?

MARSHAL. Dead sure he is.

HENRY. Did you fetch him away?

MARSHAL. Yes, I did; I brought him back in my arms, and had my guts nearly kicked into my back. It's a painful commission, bringing home the future. Do you want to see him, sir, before I take him to the Chancery?

HENRY. When he's Chancellor he can go to the Chancery.

MARSHAL. But how's this, my lord? I thought you said—

HENRY. You can go to the Chancery; you can fetch young Henry out of Becket's care, and his little wife with him.

MARSHAL. He was shaping well. Why move him?

HENRY. There's a change in the spirit of the Chancery.

MARSHAL. The boy loves the Chancellor—the Archbishop; spiritual shepherd and uncle-schoolmaster. I doubt if he'll leave the Chancery without tears. And I'm already thoroughly drenched and salted from the first one.

HENRY. We have seen the remarkable steady mind of self-love. We've nothing further to learn of that, Marshal. Fetch the boy home, and keep him in your own charge. Teach him good faith.

MARSHAL. I? Teach him?

HENRY. Good faith.

MARSHAL. I'm no schoolmaster.

HENRY. Well, then, be the book. Leave him alone to study from you.

MARSHAL [*turning to go*]. As you say.

HENRY [*his voice rising in pain*].
Tell me how a man who has seen eye to eye with me
Can suddenly look at me as if he was blind?

MARSHAL [*turning back*]. Sir?

HENRY. Fetch the boy home.

[MARSHAL *pauses for a moment as though to speak, then goes gravely away.* HENRY *slowly turns and faces the place where* BECKET *stood, as though squaring up for a fight.*

HENRY. Now . . . Becket.

CURTAIN

END OF ACT ONE

ACT TWO

ELEANOR

BECKET

HENRY

GILBERT FOLIOT

WILLIAM MARSHAL

EARL OF LEICESTER

BLAE

YOUNG HENRY, *the King's son*

RICHARD }
GEOFFREY } *his brothers*
JOHN }

ROGER, *Blae's son*

MESSENGER

BECKET'S CROSS-BEARER

BISHOPS AND MEN OF THE COURT

ACT TWO · 1163–70

BECKET, *with the* BISHOPS. *Enter* ELEANOR.

ELEANOR. I can hardly wish you Goodmorning, Archbishop,
When the morning is so unwilling to appear.
[*She bows to them, as they bow to her.*
My lords. Could you see your way across the yard?

BECKET. By groping, ma'am.

ELEANOR. Have you come to find the King?
Today's a poor day for finding any man;
Only sounds and voices, and half creations of the fog
Which move like men but fade like spirits.

BECKET. It's a murk which penetrates the flesh
And wraps round the bones. No day for the mind.

ELEANOR. Or the light foot. It's a hard, subtle terrain
You have come to cross in Henry, Becket.
Please heaven some good comes out of it.
For me (a woman who dreads an abstract passion)
It presents a chilling prospect. These London streets,
Which I seem to have to walk as a penance
For loving life too warmly, tolerate me
Less every day. And you have lost
Your genius for life, that ready sense of the world
Which used to give your gravity a charm
And your laughter a solemnity,
As though you sang the complex heart of reality
And by singing mastered it. How could worship
Or prayer do better?

BECKET. Alas, madam.

ELEANOR. Alas,
Becket!

BECKET. God must guide me.

ELEANOR. To guide the God
A little is sometimes not without merit. But I see
The only way I can have any part in life
Is to stand and be the curious onlooker
While two unproved worlds fly at each other.
Be sure you draw blood, to lift my drooping spirits.
The ground under your feet
Has become the sand of the arena.
And here's the bull you are matched with.

[ELEANOR *moves away as* HENRY *enters, with* COURTIERS.

HENRY. You had better throw some light on this new man
The Archbishop, Archbishop. We're losing precious weeks.
Every day men are born into an island
Not yet ready to receive them.
I need reassurance.

BECKET. Of what, reassurance of what?
Whether indeed there can ever be a world
Answering to the man created?

HENRY. To achieve
That is our whole concern. Suppose you tell me
How you see your own part in the process.

BECKET. To protect us from going aground on deceptive time,
To keep our course in the deep reality.
As time is contained in eternity
So is temporal action contained in eternal truth.
And that truth can't be put at the mercy of time.

HENRY. Nor time at the mercy of an ambitious Church.
I will remind you of what you know already.
There are certain customs,
Part of the growing nature of this island,
Which many generations in their need and experience
Have made their own in a common law. And these,
For what better will come of them, we mean to maintain.
You're well aware of them:
Clerics, for a crime against the common law,
To answer to the King's court.

BECKET. No doubt
You have noticed, by my wish the bishops' courts
Have made their judgements more severe.

HENRY. Very tactful and unimpressive. There have been
Already in my time a hundred murders
Which were settled by nothing but a futile fine
Or the lick of a prison.

BECKET. There would have been two hundred
If we had hanged the murderers. As it is,
There are now a hundred men who see we think
Lives of more account than they did: spirits
In trust, which we must never despair of.

HENRY. Men who make a profession of God should expect
The heavier punishment.

BECKET. They are still men.

HENRY. Indeed they are! Therefore we need to know
Who is to govern them. Let me go on.
Laymen brought up for trial before a bishop
Must be given in every instance legal witnesses.
No archbishop, bishop, or beneficed clerk
To leave the kingdom without my authority.

No one holding land of me, nor any
Minister of mine to be excommunicated
Without my knowledge. For this is what you do,
You lords of the Church Arrogant,
Like an old god crazy with his thunderbolts.
As for the rest of the problems hindering our hope,
You know them closely, having shared them.
But that was then, when I knew you. As things are,
I need your word that you'll obey these Customs.

BECKET. God said 'I am Truth', not 'I am Custom'.

HENRY. Whose truth are you, you acrobat? These Customs
Are the truth of the men whose lives shaped them.

BECKET. What a man knows he has by experience,
But what a man is precedes experience.
His experience merely reveals him, or destroys him;
Either drives him to his own negation,
Or persuades him to his affirmation, as he chooses.
And this truth is not custom.
This is not under the law, but under grace.
What you see as the freedom of the State
Within the law, I fear, as the enslavement
Of that other state of man, in which, and in
Which only, he can know his perfect freedom.
So this is how I must answer you:
We obey you in everything, unless it should threaten
The will of God, and the laws and dignity of the Church.

HENRY. 'Unless' is nothing, no answer, and no vow!
Who is to set the limit on your laws and dignity?
Who, apart from your own reading of God,
Is going to control your ambition? Very astute,
Isn't it, to attach yourself to a power
Which proceeds and communicates only through you.

BECKET. If by me you mean the Church, tell me
Who controls the ambitions of the State?

HENRY. The well-being of the whole community.
What man here will undertake
To define the will of God? We have seen it
Mauling humanity with visitations
Of horror beyond belief.
If you're so devoted to this will
Why don't you go to its aid?
Heave your house down when the hurricane shakes it,
Piss in the flood water. Strip those robes off, Becket,
And stand here shuddering
In the icy air of God's will. Or talk better sense.

BECKET. And yet here, at the mercy of these elements,
We exist more often unharmed.
The vehement liberty of terror, which ignores our flesh,
Is not the will,
But it knows the will, returns to it in calm.
Even when in rebellion it keeps
The signature of light. In the avalanche of snow
The star-figure of the flake is there unchanged.
It was out of a whirlwind that God answered Job.
And here, too, in the whirl of our senses,
The way for this will has to be kept unthreatened.

HENRY. The will of the people is the will of God.

BECKET. They have many wills: many lusts and many thirsts:
A will for death as well as a will for life.
But, quick or dormant, in th'm they have a longing
To be worked into the eternal fabric
By God's love. And so we go with you faithfully,
And swear we will, only saving our order.

HENRY. Which means whatever you like to make it.
One order is going to be saved: mine in this kingdom!
You know as well as I do, your saving clause
Is more effective than what you swear. You, Foliot,
Give me a straighter answer. You, you, you, you!
You're not so brash in your calling.

FOLIOT. Well, my lord,
We are here as one body. It will have to be
As the Church is led to reply: in everything
Obedient saving our order.

A BISHOP. Obedient
Saving our order.

OTHERS. Saving our order. Our order.
[HENRY'*s anger is like an explosion of madness.*

HENRY [*with a roar*].
Save your commonsense if you want to stay as you are!
The Church never said this to a King before.
By God, it's not going to begin with me!
I had a demon for an ancestor.
There are times I feel her wading in my blood and howling
For a sacrifice of obscurantical fools.
And by God, she shall have it!
Your old immunity is over, you're trapped
In a change of the world, my lords, which men deserve
And are going to be given. The man who gets in the way
Is of no more consequence than a skull
Kicked about by oafs in a field,
And that's what he will come to. Jesus whipped!
You have reason to blench and hug your skirts round you,
I'll tear the parts out of you—
Hell doesn't have a monopoly in torment.

You will find as good here, if you pull your pious faces
When I ask for help. You'd better consider it.

[*He leaves them in an uproar. An unnatural light begins to penetrate the fog. Faces are distorted by it. Shadows gesticulate at a great height above the* MEN *of the Court, who rage against the* PRIESTS, *some advancing towards them waving axes. The* BISHOPS *harry* BECKET *in extreme anxiety.*

THE COURT [*the words that can be heard*].
Time it was said! They've got to learn where they live. They've got a hold on the country beyond anything ever known. Grabbing lands that haven't been theirs for a generation. Making us a property of Rome. [*They advance on the* BISHOPS, *some waving axes*:] Consider, if you want to live. We'll split your heads open and find your brains! If the road wants clearing, here's a cleaver to do it. That's it, beat a retreat! Ah yes, now you know the times you live in!

[*At the same time the* BISHOPS *have moved crying out to* BECKET.]

BISHOPS. Have you thought where you lead us? How do we serve the Church if we lose our Sees? Or our lives, perhaps: God knows what he intends. You've lost us the friendship of the King. The Holy Father said Be moderate; moderate, he said, moderate. If you had shown a spark of your old will to please. . . . Is your power to leave you, now you're powerful?

COURTIER. Take your time, Archbishop. The King's in dead earnest.

BECKET. As I am.

COURT. What becomes of your influence if you rot out your life in a dungeon, nobody even remembering where you are? And are you so sure of your motives, with due respect, my lord? No self-applause, no vainglory, no obstinacy? Anyway, your future, and the Church's too, depends on the way you think.

A BISHOP. Have you thought of our distress?

BECKET [*suddenly, after silence*]. Where is the King?

ELEANOR. Ask yourself where it is you stand, saying
Where is the King?
Look round at the unreality of the light
And the unreality of the faces in the light.
You and he, you told him, would reach a place
Where you might not know what was being made of you,
Or understand the conclusion when it came.
Certainly the familiar world has departed.
A death-world here, where every move
Is magnified on to the fog's blind face
And becomes the gesture of a giant.

A BISHOP. You made your decision alone. Carry it alone.

[*Enter* HENRY. *He stands in the strange light, looking at* BECKET. *All other eyes are also on* BECKET.

BECKET. Still with anxiety, but hoping, trusting
That you mean to command nothing against my conscience,
I will give you the Yes you ask for.

[*An exhalation of relief from the* BISHOPS.

HENRY. Then we can go ahead. What do the rest say?

FOLIOT. Yes; in good faith.

BISHOPS. In good faith. Good faith.

HENRY. You are men of admirable judgement.
Here they are, the Customs of the kingdom,
Codified, ready for your seal. And when it's done
You can give us a burst of bell-ringing to clear the air.

BECKET. What's this?

HENRY. Your word made parchment. Fifteen paragraphs;
You're familiar with all of them.

ELEANOR [*to herself*]. A false move.
Oh, never define!

BECKET. No! By all-prevailing
God: no! I'll never set my seal to this.

HENRY. Ah!

BECKET [*to the* BISHOPS]. You see where being accommodating
And afraid has brought us. Fear is the father of sin,
The devil's best weapon is a man's nerves!

HENRY. He agrees
To cramming God into the words of dogma,
But evades the simple expression of law!

BECKET [*to the* BISHOPS]. You see
The pit that's dug for us under the spread branches.
Dreading that I should be cast out and alone
I was leading the Church to a broken back,
Betraying all heaven's charge that was trusted in me:
A poverty of spirit please God I never
Approach again. Harder the forgiveness
Which I now need to find. For now indeed
I'm alone. The knowledge of my fault
Is my only companion. [*He moves away.*

FOLIOT [*in despair*]. Where are you leaving us?
Fairly lying between the hammer and the anvil!

HENRY. Now you begin to know him, the bewildering
Turns to maintain himself, first will, then won't:
Will in the abstract, won't in the definition.
He pretends to agree, to mask his real intentions,
Until his bluff is called. And now we're to have
A display of the anguished penitent
While he looks for a way out. But I shall help him
To bring order to this disarray of the spirit.

You reject your work as Chancellor. I'll relieve you
Of all shadow of that great and false expense.
You needn't be haunted by a sense of debt
Which might hamper your independence.
You shall pay me back every penny you received
From the estates and castles which were yours then.

BECKET [*turning*]. But you freed me from all secular obligations
The day I was consecrated.

HENRY. Before you freed
Yourself from the purpose of the time you live in.
You will make good the sums you spent
On your war in Toulouse.

BECKET. In the service of the State!

HENRY. It was in the service of recommending Becket
To himself and me.

BECKET. It will somehow be paid.

HENRY [*now in full cry*].
And since the eternal account overlooks nothing,
To free your conscience by precise audit
You can pay the country back what you had from all
The vacant sees and abbeys while you were Chancellor.
Then devote yourself to God with a less hang-dog look.

[*A moan of consternation from the* BISHOPS. BECKET *falls on one knee, and supports himself with a hand on the floor, like a pugilist waiting to rise before the end of the count.*

FOLIOT. Have you given yourself time, my lord,
To think what this means? Where will the Archbishop
Find the sureties for so much? Do you mean
To punish us all, to shake the whole spiritual power?

HENRY. Who will not be glad to share a burden
Which lightens a bowed conscience? The Archbishop

Prefers to abandon the things of this world. [*His anger returns.*]
Why should a man make God my enemy
And the enemy of a maturing nation,
As this man does? You shall see him as I found him:
A man depending on office, no nearer God
Than I am. Tell him to come back and face me.

CLERIC. Sir, he is ill, the Archbishop; he has to ask you
To excuse him; he is taken ill.

HENRY. Contempt
Of the royal summons! He piles up his mistakes.
The more he squirms to free himself, the more
He tangles himself in guilt. Twice already
During the last month or two he has tried
To get to France without my authority,
And twice the ships have brought him back again.
It looks as if this island
Isn't large enough to contain both of us.

ELEANOR [*to herself*].
Who will grow large enough to contain the island?

HENRY. Either there are laws for every man,
And he is one; or there are no laws for any man.
The day is vital, and the world can't stand still
To be cheated, even under cover of God.

ELEANOR. Let me say this to the man who makes the world—
And also to the man who makes himself the Church.
Consider complexity, delight in difference.
Fear, for God's sake, your exact words.
Do you think you can draw lines on the living water?
Together we might make a world of progress.
Between us, by our three variants of human nature,
You and Becket and me, we could be

The complete reaching forward. Neither of you
Will dare to understand it. Have I spoken too late?

HENRY [*ignoring her*]. The issue is so great, the man so intractable,
It has come to this; he has to stand his trial,
And be judged by England, not by me,
By England's dawning knowledge of herself,
As though she tried herself in the trial of Becket.
We have done with privilege of person. None of us
Is anything more than the purpose of our time.
[*He leaves, in the diminishing light.*

ELEANOR. Who has left the most blood on the sand, Marshal?

MARSHAL. Ma'am, the Archbishop is badly gored, that's certain. But what wounds have been made on the King we still have to discover. This business has grown too big for me.

ELEANOR. Grown very small, Marshal: the size of two men in a rage.
We are not going to see the great issues contending,
Nor the new spirit of England being forged in a fire.
We shall see the kicks and blows of angry men,
Both losing sight of the cause.
The high names
Of God and the State are now displaced
By hurt pride, self-distrust, foiled ambition,
And the rest of our common luggage.

MARSHAL. That may be. But, all the same, the Archbishop is on trial.

ELEANOR. When the glorious battle turns into the vendetta
The great issues, no longer controlled by men,
Themselves take over command. Then at last he may listen
To some other voice than his own!

MARSHAL. You mean the King?

ELEANOR. You saw, Marshal, how he turned away from me?
Am I no more distinct than the men who walk in the fog?
If I think I am a woman of flesh and blood,
And unmistakeable spirit,
He will soon undeceive me. He turned away
As he would from his shadow on the wall.

MARSHAL. But, ma'am—

ELEANOR. Go to him, Marshal: love him as you can.
He will have need of that. [*Exit* ELEANOR.

[*When the light returns,* FOLIOT *and another* BISHOP *are standing at one side. Enter* BECKET *with his cross-bearer* ALEXANDER LLEWELYN. *He takes the cross from* LLEWELYN.

FOLIOT. Look at this. Does he know what he's doing? [*To* BECKET.] You're ill advised, aren't you, Archbishop, to come here carrying your own cross? It's like drawing a sword out of the scabbard in the King's face. Suppose he should draw his own sword in reply? We should see a country at war with itself.

BECKET. We should know a man at war with himself. That's a risk we have to commit to God.

[*He goes forward, using the cross as a staff in his left hand, as the* EARL OF LEICESTER *enters. He stops short as he sees* BECKET *advancing to take his seat.* BECKET *sits.*

FOLIOT [*to the* BISHOP].
A fool he was, and a fool he always will be.

BECKET [*to* LEICESTER].
What do you have to say to me? What is it?

LEICESTER. The verdict of the trial.

BECKET. Such you call it.

LEICESTER. My lord, time has never seen before

Such a council as this, representing a whole nation
Sitting with the King in a conclave of law;
The evidence argued and weighed with deep anxiety.
And this new coherence of justice finds you
A perjurer and the King's traitor.

BECKET. Have you surrendered your mind so completely
That you can believe in this use of law?
Judgement is a sentence given after trial.
I was brought here on a pretext, not a charge.
So, for all your threshing of documents, the King
Thumbing his way through the always altering Customs,
Sweating for precedents and legal justification,
There has been no trial. And no trial can have no sentence.

LEICESTER. All you possess you hold from the King.

BECKET. Nothing. Nothing from the King. Whatever the Church
Holds is held in perpetual liberty.
I am your father, though you hold me in disdain:
Still and always your father, however vexed in thought,
Fallible in action, unpersuading in word,
Falling short in everything that makes
A man convince his times with truth. In spite
Of all, your father; and by a father's authority
I forbid you to give sentence.

LEICESTER. Do I take
This answer to the King?

BECKET. There is nothing
To be answered. I leave here as I came.

[BECKET *moves away, bearing the cross, in a storm of threats and mocks from those of the* COURT *who are present. As* LEICESTER *turns to go, enter* HENRY.

HENRY. Where has he gone?

LEICESTER. He goes as he came, he said,
Refusing sentence, denying any trial.

HENRY. Fetch him back. We haven't done with him yet.

MARSHAL [*coming forward*].
This isn't the time to pursue him.
Three-quarters of the town followed him here,
And those who could, got down on their knees
And kissed the step he came in by. Take a look.
He can hardly get away or control his horse.

HENRY. There you have the measure of these people.
You can labour night and day to give them
A world that's comprehensible.
But their idolatry goes to any man—
Though he reeks of fault and cares less about their lives
Than he does for a point of heresy so fine
It wouldn't shake a hair in God's nostril—
So long as they think he bargains with a world beyond them.
Well, let them have his blessing,
Drawn with two fingers on the air.
I shall still bless them better in their daily lives;
And God can hear me and make the best of it.

Enter ELEANOR

ELEANOR. Other men have been busy with the ear of God.
There's news from Paris.

HENRY. Tonight he can lie
On his bed, and heave his breast with a sense
Of mastery which in fact is finished.

ELEANOR. Over how many years, I wonder,
Has Louis been pestering heaven for a male heir.
How many saints have been dragged from the calendar
To intervene? Almost a year ago

He lay flat on the chancel floor, refusing
To get up again until the Chapter had promised
To combine in one great assault of prayer.

HENRY. What is the news from Paris?

ELEANOR. The power of prayer
Is the news from Paris. It has come in a letter
Written by Gerald of Wales three nights ago.
He was working late, he said, and had just put
His philosophy-fuddled head on to the pillow
When the frame of his bed began to shake
With a vibration of bells from every church in the city.
His dark room was all of a sudden
Staggering with torchlight. So he dived for his shirt
And made for the window. The whole of Paris was out
Streaming westwards. The prayers have reached their mark.

HENRY. It has taken them twenty years to get there.

ELEANOR. When he called from the window for news, an old woman
Waved a burning torch under his chin.
'Watch out for yourself,' she said,
'A king's been born in Paris tonight
'Who is going to be a hammer to your king of England!'—
So even the bricks and haycocks in France are dancing.
The child has got into their wine.

HENRY. They'd better make the most of it. He may die yet.

ELEANOR. They have called him Philip-Augustus, Dieu-Donné,
Given by God on an August night; hinting,
What's more, at empire, a name full of promise.

[HENRY *turns to the men of the* COURT.

HENRY. You can all go to your beds.
Except you, Marshal; bring Foliot here.

[HENRY *and* ELEANOR *alone.*

HENRY. You're pleased with the news from Paris.

ELEANOR. When heaven makes one of its rare rejoinders
I should have thought it the merest common civility
For all of us to attempt a smile.

HENRY. It's a smile against everything we've succeeded in.

ELEANOR. I smile however I am moved to smile.

HENRY. Even at the prospect of a troubled future.

ELEANOR. You haven't left my mind much else to do,
Except appreciate
Life's more acid comments on human endeavour.
And then I smile. Tell me, in fact,
What place do I have in your perfect order?
You served me, and your posterity is safe.
So much for you and me. And now I am nothing in this land,
Nothing but your occasional whore.
I have been a legend. What is left of that now?
You expect me to abandon
The inheritance of brain and heart
Which I received from my ancestors,
Who for generations have been a race of men
Born to act on events like sun on the vine.
But before the vows of marriage I accepted the vows
Of birth and blood. I shall be as faithful to mine
As you are to yours, though yours are lawless:
You who so struggle for order everywhere
Except in your own life.
If anarchy should prove to be a state which is indivisible,
Stretching from your own body across the face of the world,
You have stinging days ahead of you. Meanwhile
I smile, at this and that; and the boy born to France.

HENRY. The future of the young eagles means nothing to you.

ELEANOR. Does it not? I am their mother.

HENRY. And I'm their father,
However at odds I may be with time and men;
However beset within and without, I am still
Their father; and your birth and blood
To which you say you intend to be true, mingle there
With mine. God above us, the house is a single thing!

ELEANOR. Though no man in the kingdom has enough fingers
To count your women: and all men know what tunes
You play on that Welsh harp, Rosamund de Clifford.
[*Sings to herself.*] 'By the flowing river a flower is growing.
'In a Thames bower gleams the king's own flower.
'Rosamunda, Rosamund, rose of the world . . .'
Curious I should forget how that song goes on. I hear it so often, when the wind's my way; though usually whistled.

Re-enter WILLIAM MARSHAL, *with* GILBERT FOLIOT.

HENRY. There's nothing to be said. The days are hot;
The thirst on the way demands a little shade
And fresh water. One thing I ask you to remember—

ELEANOR. You sent for London. Here he is. [*Exit* ELEANOR.

HENRY. The labouring is most dark alone. Foliot,
There's a boy for France.

MARSHAL. I told him.

FOLIOT. I had heard.

HENRY. The scrap of flesh has given them a future.
France from now on has a new pair of eyes in its head.
We have to make sure those eyes look out on a future
Already decided, an established world.

FOLIOT. What man dictates the future?

HENRY. In this instance, I do. We'll put it in working order.
Young Harry can have the crown of England now.

MARSHAL. Two kings at once?

HENRY. We'll plant the saplings firmly in their place.
All the boys shall have their lands, and learn
To love and defend them while I am alive to see it.
Richard can have Poitou and Aquitaine.

FOLIOT. The Queen's lands!

HENRY. Richard is the boy most hers; her lands
Fall naturally to him.

MARSHAL. Think a moment, sir; we know the young princes
Have a sight more vigour than experience.
What do you think they will make of a gift of power
Like this which you mean to give them?

HENRY. Nothing but good,
Because the voice of Plantagenet is one voice,
Calling and answering along the same road.
The power I give them is trust and affection. How
Can this be ill spent?

FOLIOT. Do you think the Archbishop
Will be prepared to crown the boy?

HENRY. What Archbishop?—It shall be done as I say.
Come on, we can discuss when and how. Do you see
The bated look the sky has? The way of the wind
Is altering. The trees are drawn with chalk on slate.
Spit in the air, Foliot. You will see how differently
The world looks in the morning when its plan
Is well drawn for a hundred years of peace.

[*Exeunt* HENRY *and* FOLIOT.

MARSHAL. But the morning was only another day. It emerged sullen and bedraggled, after a night of bucketing rain, much as we all did after a night of too little sleep. I heard the chanting of Compline, then of Mattins, and at last of Lauds. And the daylight was hard to face.

Enter TWO MONKS

1ST MONK. What is the news of him? How does he do, the Archbishop?

2ND MONK. He does very well. He has left us. So it goes.

1ST MONK. Is dead, do you mean?

2ND MONK. As far as the King's concerned, worse than dead. Last night one of the town gates was left unlocked, by the greased palm of a miracle. And heaven took the chance, and produced a storm of rain to cover up the sound of his riding away.

1ST MONK. He's out of the King's hands, then?

2ND MONK. Out of the King's hands, nearly out of the kingdom: disguised, heading for the coast; making for the French court. So it goes.

MARSHAL. Before noon the whispers had become a certainty. Before a month was over, Louis, to all Europe, was the man who protected the Kingdom of God, and Henry the man who was trying to destroy it.

1ST MONK. Thank God he is free.

2ND MONK. Thank God, if you like, for a father who deserts his children. That's the state we are in now.

1ST MONK. What are we to think of it, then?

2ND MONK. There is a toll to be paid to the devil on any road a man takes.

MARSHAL. As the day went on, the streets were choked with rumours. The man Becket was at large and the world rocked.—

But the King made his way as before, forcing new roads ahead of him. . . . There were other things to concern us. Today we've crowned the dark secret of the future. The young eagles are coming into their inheritance.

Enter BLAE

I was looking for you, sweetheart.

BLAE. Well, look who's here.

MARSHAL. I've brought you one of the new coins: struck to celebrate young Henry's coronation.

BLAE. How much more is it worth than the old ones?

MARSHAL. Not a ha'penny, but it's an interesting object. If you want to see them come back from the Abbey and take a look at your boy, I'll show you a place where you can squint through into the hall. [*He leads her to a point of vantage.*

BLAE [*as she goes*]. Thanks. I'd like to see him again. How is he growing?

MARSHAL. Not altogether up, but he thickens; and what he hasn't got in inches he piles on in intelligence. He sits at his books like a man who would rather eat paper than beef.

BLAE. Ah, God, that's the strange thing! To think that though I never had a brain in my head I once had those brains in my belly.

MARSHAL. The King means to have him for his Chancellor.

BLAE. Well, you never know what will come of your guts.

Trumpets. Enter, as from the Coronation, YOUNG HENRY, GEOFFREY, RICHARD, *and* JOHN, *his brothers*; BLAE'*s son* ROGER *and* HENRY *and* ELEANOR.

MARSHAL. Here they come now.

BLAE. That's not him, is it? No, that's not him, I know.

MARSHAL. That's the young prince Geoffrey, Count of Brittany by the new mandate. . . . And there's Richard: sings like a minstrel: his mother's boy.

BLAE. There's Roger now; I know him, I know my boy!

MARSHAL. There he is. He keeps a dogged, patient kind of manner, considering the provocation he gets from the four legitimates.

BLAE. He's a man on the way all right, God bless him. I didn't do half bad there. That's a thought worth keeping to end my days with.

[MARSHAL *leaves her and joins the Court. As the stage fills,* BLAE *is lost to view.*

HENRY. So I've seen beyond my death; what other man
Can say that? Blessed to rest, if only for a moment,
On the days which won't be my concern. And then
It was good, that passing salute of the sun
As we came out on the street.

ELEANOR. And the sighing silence
Of the crowd who saw it.

[*They go aside to disrobe.* MARSHAL *kneels to* YOUNG HENRY.

MARSHAL. My loyalty, for all the days I live.

YOUNG HENRY. There's not likely to come a time when I shall doubt it.

HENRY. Help him off with his robes.

YOUNG HENRY. No; I'll wear them.

RICHARD. He has the illusion of being a king, Marshal;
Don't disabuse him.

YOUNG HENRY. Brother Richard is having
A morning of envy.

RICHARD. Says the shadow of his dad.

HENRY [*raising a cup*].
A long and prosperous life to Harry, to keep
The flower of the broom golden when I'm gone.
Pledge him, Richard,
And you, Geoffrey. John, the health of your brother.

RICHARD. Prosperity, if you can get it.

GEOFFREY. And good endeavour
To our wives, to hurry on the generations:
Especially to mine. Much pleasure to Constance.

JOHN. I shall reign before your children.

GEOFFREY. Will you, sprat?
You mean to live as long as that, do you?

ELEANOR. A long life to all my defiant eagles.

[HENRY *sets refreshment before* YOUNG HENRY.

HENRY. May all men serve you well, and you them.

MARSHAL. Not many princes are given the dignity
Of being served by a king.

YOUNG HENRY. If Becket had been there to crown me
I should have known what my dignity was worth.

GEOFFREY. Good health to the troublesome Archbishop!

[*A moment of silence. Except for a quick movement from* ROGER *towards the* KING, *no one moves, until the* KING, *while* MARSHAL *is speaking, swings round on the Court and dismisses them.*

MARSHAL. Each time he made a bold move to clear the way ahead, the ground became more dangerous than ever. When he thought he had finally disposed of Becket, the name of Becket was breathed out like fire all over Christendom. And now, when with love and trust, he stations the boys as sentinels to the Angevin world, the ground seems to crack where he stands.

YOUNG HENRY. Why shouldn't we speak of Becket. I am very fond of him.

GEOFFREY. He does very well in France, I hear: hand-in-glove with Louis.

YOUNG HENRY. They know how to value a man there, that's the truth.

RICHARD. What do you put your value at, lord high brother? I'll knock you down for a song.

HENRY. Good patience, do I have to plead with you
To think where your own interest lies?
Whoever makes harm for me harms you, and all
Those thousands of lives who look to us
For their safe conduct across time. We are bound
In one future, each depending on the others.

ELEANOR. And yet, you can no more make the future obey you
Than you can make yourself obey
Your own belief in the just mind.
Haven't you just driven out of your kingdom
Four hundred human lives, men, women, children,
In the middle of winter, out over a wild sea
With nowhere to go?—And their crime, what is their crime?
Simply their relationship to Becket.

YOUNG HENRY. Is this what he has done?

ELEANOR. They have gone to France, to spread the gospel
Of our just law-giving master of government,
To whose unknown fate my sons have been dedicated.

HENRY. To a strong peace in which they can thrive.

ELEANOR. You have set half Europe raging to see you brought down.
I will tell you something certain about the future.
You will be alone. You have given my lands to Richard,

As though you considered me already dead.
It shall be so, then: to you I will be dead.
My life is in Poitou with Richard. There
At least, the warm sun will give me leave to smile.
And we shall make laws for sport and love
And put a little light in the eyes of Europe.

RICHARD. With three thousand men-at-arms at my disposal.

YOUNG HENRY. You caretaker of your mother's lands!

ELEANOR. You shall come to us there, Harry, all of you shall come,
Whenever you make yourselves your own masters,
Or when you need the sun to set your blood
Flowing more freely than ever it can here.

HENRY. That evil genius they called you once
Is alive again: turns now towards these boys.

ELEANOR. They shall show me how the world should be.
And I will believe there can be such a world.

HENRY. You were with me all through the time when I was shaping
The nightmare into an empire. Do you mean
To give the nightmare back to them? You can remember it.

ELEANOR. I know it still. But at last
I mean to wrench myself awake
And open my eyes to my own reality.

HENRY. Then please God you find that dawn less false
Than it is to me. Your true reality
Is in guarding what I have made.

ELEANOR. It's in myself, past, present, and to come.
Where will they find yours? They will break you open to find it.
[*Exit* ELEANOR. *The boys glance at one another.*

YOUNG HENRY. There are too many things wrong here
In the old world of your generation, father.

Hardly any content with the way things are going.
I have ears; I know what's going on.

[RICHARD *gives a deflating twang on an instrument. There is silence for a moment.*

HENRY. Sons,
Look well into the human face.
You will see there the desert you must cross
If you mean to make the city. God knows
At first I could have believed all men
Were born of an act of love, though sometimes
To be contended with, or destroyed, or wept over,
Yet never altogether losing the trace
Of the good hunger which made them. Now there aren't
Many I can look at with much belief.
But, by Christ's blood, I'll give them the city of the law
Even if I have to make it by fearful means.
And then trust it complete into your hands,
Which are also of my making.
But first look well into the human face. [*Exit* HENRY.

RICHARD [*strumming*]. 'So then they all to dinner went
Upon a carpet green . . .'
Do Harry; visit us in Poitou
When your crown starts to cut into your forehead.

YOUNG HENRY. I can see it's been cutting into yours all day.

RICHARD [*leaning towards him*]. Now look again: a flawless brow.
[*He tips* YOUNG HENRY'*s crown.*] But what
Do we see here? It's the mark of the royal slavey.

GEOFFREY. Show him respect, Dick. You can still smell the holy oil on him. Sing him the song you made for the coronation.

RICHARD. What is music to a man who has lost his liberty?
Well, we can try.

[*sings*] To sing of a woman is no care.
Only to mention breasts, belly, and thighs
Is to have the music.
Or sing of no more than her hair,
The moist lips, the closing eyes,
And there, there
Are the words and the air.

But praising a brother for a crown
Which no more fits him than a basin,
It's hard to do it.
A shadow with a royal frown—
What notes will fill the diapason?
And where, where
Are the—

[YOUNG HENRY *leaps up and grabs the instrument.*

YOUNG HENRY. All right, I've stood enough!

RICHARD. Afraid of the truth?

YOUNG HENRY. Fed up with insolence and envy. I'll settle with you. [*He takes off his crown and robes.*

GEOFFREY. Oh, this is excellent! There's war among us!

RICHARD. Less arduous than making songs. Look, what ferocity!

[*They draw their swords.* JOHN *puts on the robes and the crown, which are too large for him.*

JOHN. I'll be the king.

YOUNG HENRY. I'm ready for you; come on.

RICHARD. Pleasure, pleasure, pleasure.

[GEOFFREY *has also taken a sword, and is ready to signal the start of the fight.* ROGER, *who has stood silently by until now, suddenly speaks.*

ROGER. Don't be such fools. Put the swords away.

RICHARD. Ding, dang.

GEOFFREY. Their blood's up. Now we really have come into our inheritance. Mother Mary, this is very interesting.

[He starts the fight with a lift of his sword. ROGER *gets between the fighting brothers. Unnoticed, he is wounded.*

ROGER. I tell you, you're not going to go on with this!

RICHARD. Look out, you bastard boy, we're busy.

YOUNG HENRY. Have you lost your senses? Get away from here.

GEOFFREY. Cut off his legs and continue.

YOUNG HENRY. Come over here, Dick.

ROGER. It's nothing to me if you want to slide about on your own blood.

YOUNG HENRY. Then get out of the way.

ROGER. Except that it's my blood too, at least in part,
But, aside from that, it's the blood of the whole body
Of Plantagenet government; of the world's peace,
And the outcome of everything the king has lived for.
What thought have you given to that? What other man
Living could have gone so ahead of his time,
Holding so steadily to what he believes in,
While envy, prejudice, and self-interest
Are disputing every step he goes? And now
You can't keep the peace among yourselves! I tell you
If you don't know how to combine in one Plantagenet will
You might as well trundle the crown straight into the sea!

RICHARD. We'll show you how we combine to deal with a pompous, impertinent ass!

GEOFFREY. Is the new King subdued by a cocky little bastard? . . . Look out.

[He has seen HENRY *and* MARSHAL *returning.*

ROGER. I seem to have taken . . . a cut from the swords . . . when I . . . [*He falls. The three sons, with swords drawn, stand in a semi-circle around* ROGER.

YOUNG HENRY. It wasn't any fault of ours. He got in the way.

GEOFFREY. A burst of oratory knocked him down. Well, we're very sorry.

MARSHAL [*kneeling by* ROGER]. Quite a scratch here; he's been losing blood. All right, he's coming round.

HENRY. So you mean to carry out the prophecy:
From the devil we came, and to the devil we'll go—
Brother against brother, the sons against the father.
I thought we might have got free from that curse.

GEOFFREY. Nobody was going to kill anybody, as far as I know.

[RICHARD *goes off, strumming the instrument;* GEOFFREY *with him.* JOHN *leaves the crown and robes beside* YOUNG HENRY, *who remains.* MARSHAL *has helped* ROGER *to his feet, but he loses consciousness again and* MARSHAL *picks him up in his arms.*

MARSHAL. It's not so long ago that I carried him here
Struggling like a bat in a veil. No serious
Damage is done that I see. [*Exit* MARSHAL.

HENRY. But how much
That none of you see.

YOUNG HENRY. What else could I have done?
Sit like a girl and let them mock at the crown?
They were trying to make a laughing-stock of me,
Said I was nothing but your shadow.
But I can make men follow me, and command them, too,
And strike fire out of my name as good as any
Or better.

HENRY. You can find men to follow you:
All the malcontents, hangers-on and family runts:
They would follow you, if your brains were pig-swill.
But if you want better than that, wait until time
Has made something of you. As it is
You're not fit to lead a crusade of children.

[YOUNG HENRY *puts his head in his hands.*

Harry, have you never heard men mock at me,
With a contempt for what I do, enlarging
The errors, belittling the purpose, refusing
To nourish the attempt; for all they're worth
Increasing the chance of failure? When the world
Laughs at its own opinion of you
Don't let it destroy
The man you are going to become.

YOUNG HENRY. They shall see what I am.

[*He takes his robes and crown and goes out, past* MARSHAL, *who enters.*

MARSHAL. He is in good hands. He will soon recover.

HENRY. I wish I could say the same of everything about us.
But the days have been lamed, Marshal, somewhere in the mind.
We may have to go on with that to the end now.
Why do I see that arc of drawn swords
And the falling body as though they would never leave me?
Am I losing heart? Good man, that's not the trouble yet.
I can go further and harder than we've come.
But the health has gone out of the air.

MARSHAL. Sir, you remember at St. David's when you came
To the great stone across the river, the woman
Who screamed out at you Merlin's prophecy
That the King would die as he walked across the stone.
You hesitated; but you crossed.

HENRY [*chuckling*]. With my feet
On Merlin's reputation. Right enough, Marshal,
We shall reach the other side. You shall see
How we change the look of things. The whole of Europe
Is snarling at us, yes? Louis up in arms
And off to invade Normandy, on the understanding
That our day is over! Right! Now, Marshal,
Observe the transformation. Henry Plantagenet
Is in the mood for wooing. Our disturbing spirit
Is prepared to humble itself,
To cool the hot bellies, making such a gusty
Rumble of indignation. Louis for a start:
Catch him in Normandy, wake him up to see me
There beside him, like his first shadow in the morning.

MARSHAL. Already he thinks you don't travel as other men do,
But go on wings.

HENRY. Carrying persuasion, I hope.
'Why, Louis, my liege, this won't do.
'I've brought sad confusion to your mind,
'Which my sorrow will mend. You who know so well
'The extent of divine mercy, will want to see
'A reconciliation between Becket and me.
'I promise him a safe return to England
'And full possession of his office; and he can crown
'Young Harry all over again, with his and your
'Young Margaret.'—And so we steady the days
And begin to cross the stone, Marshal.

MARSHAL. And how
Does the aggrieved heart of the Archbishop take it?

HENRY. Look, Marshal: I am going half way to meet him.
And here we stand in Normandy, ready to float him
Again towards England. And God knows I have shown him

Plenty of reverence—
Holding his stirrup for him while he dismounts,
Acknowledging that the less should serve the greater—
Louis could hardly do better.
And before God I would have things as they were.
I only ask him to treat me with tolerable respect
In front of these men who are watching us from their places.
[MEN *are standing behind. Enter* BECKET.
Let us show each other all the good we can
And forget our quarrel.

BECKET. I am very willing.

HENRY. The days behind us are thoroughly rebuked.
If we ever remember them
It will be with such fierce pain, the days ahead
Will double their virtue to overcome it.
There have been many kings of England before me,
Some greater, some less than I am. And many good
And holy Archbishops. Behave to me as the most
Holy of your predecessors behaved
To the least of mine, I'll be satisfied.

BECKET. I am touched by this. Yet we mustn't forget
That if our predecessors had settled everything well
We should never have had to undergo
These fearful years, of such harm to us both.

HENRY. Maybe so. Also remembering
That providence is a great maker of journeys,
And whoever refuses to go forward is dropped by the road.

BECKET. At least I take hopefully to the sea with you;
And surely England will take us up
Like a palm-branch in its hand, to see us riding
Together again on the road to London.

HENRY. Well, that must wait till I come there.

BECKET [*a pause*]. Does this mean
I'm returning alone?

HENRY. I can't come yet.
A little time will be yours to find your place again.

BECKET. This isn't the homecoming I expected.

HENRY. Your old weakness for riding in triumph, Becket.
I have to disappoint you. But if we go on soberly
The day for redeeming the past won't be far off.

BECKET. I pray it may come. But looking towards England now
Something tells me I am parting from you
As one you may see no more in this life.

HENRY. Heaven forgive us, do you think I intend
Any treachery to you?

BECKET. May it be a long way from your wish.
But sometimes in the mind's despair
When every thought and contrary thought, every
Act and opposing act, equally bear some taint
Of the man I am, I see I may be one of those
Whose life won't serve.

HENRY. Don't be too proud to live.
What's the matter with you? Can't you trust yourself
To accept the promise of things improving?—Becket,
The sea is running as smooth as a hound for you;
I'm sending you back with a pliant wind
All in your favour. And, if everything goes as it should,
You shall have the kiss of peace when I come to England.
Is this intention good enough to be blessed?

BECKET. In the name of Triune Majesty, the blessing
Of heaven on you.

HENRY. And mine of the world on you.

[*Exit* BECKET.

MARSHAL. It isn't the blessing of the world he's after now,
Nor yours; he is trying to find a success
Beyond human argument.

HENRY. Looking
Into his eyes, Marshal, I could find nothing there
Which could help us to a new beginning. He makes me despair.

MARSHAL. Thinking back on it now, he seemed to me like a man
Who had gone through life saving up all passion
To spend at last on his own downfall.
What else are we to think, when we remember
How he behaved as soon as he reached England?
If that wasn't infatuation, that clumsy, aggressive
Unforbearance, before his shoes were dry
From the foam of the beach, there's no more charitable word.
I shall never forget the Bishop of London's face
When he brought us the first news of it.
He came pitching to Normandy, like a leap to safety.

Enter GILBERT FOLIOT

FOLIOT. It has been even worse than I feared it would be.
His rapturous welcome at Dover, and all the way
To Canterbury, so buoyed him up,
He might have been the lord of Spring
Making his progress on the winter roads.
Not a happy beginning to help him to moderation.
And as soon as a roof was over him, he struck
His note, in his most uncompromising key.
Excommunication for all who took part
In the crowning. And your men and his, my lord,
Had already clashed with some loss of life even before I left.

HENRY. I put him in the way of peace.

FOLIOT. You will never have it in his lifetime!

HENRY [*raging*].
What's the good of any of you, standing round
Like a lot of rotting pit-props, while you leave me
Wide open to the insolence of a fellow
Who came to me first on a limping mule, and now
Might as well spread his buttocks on the throne?
Do you all intend to sit about for ever
With your hands hanging slack between your knees,
Leaving him to foul the whole distance we've covered?
Who will get rid of this turbulent priest for me?
Are you all such feeble lovers of the kingdom?

[FOUR MEN, *silently touching and beckoning each other, leave the stage.*

FOLIOT [*disturbed*].
I may have spoken with too much bitterness.
My world is too recently shaken to see these things
In a prudent light, but that is what we must do
With God's help; as we tried, my colleagues and I,
To nurse him through the dangers of his temperament,
Hoping for wisdom. And in return for this
He cuts us out of the Church's body like tumours.
But I know I spoke with too much feeling.

HENRY [*cool again*].
And great relish. We can take to the counsel-table,
Consider soberly the best way to move against him.
He has made his last mistake, and exempted me
From any promise I made to forget the past.
As he insists on being the sickness of the kingdom
It's up to us to be the physicians, to diagnose

The sickness, consult, and cure.
[*He turns and sees the empty places.*
What has become
Of the men who were with us?

FOLIOT. I was half aware of their going, that's true, and felt
A passing fear that your words might have been given
A more violent meaning than you meant to give them.

HENRY. What words of mine? You have some damnable thought.
What the devil do you mean?

MARSHAL. You may have more devoted men about you
Than you knew, or men with a devotion
To work off some score of their own, only waiting
For the first excuse to show their love for the kingdom.

HENRY. But they have no love for me! Neither have you
To have let them go. They had no permission to withdraw!
This was your doing, not mine, Foliot.
Get after them, Marshal; set men riding
On every road to the coast, search every port
And ship, and bring the lunatics back
If you kill your horses! [MARSHAL *and others hurry away.*
I swear before God
This wasn't what I meant! It was not what I meant.
Go and pray; have the pain of prayer
Harsher than you have ever known it.

FOLIOT. I'm convinced we shall see them back, my lord.

HENRY. Convince your knees to pray until we know the answer.
[FOLIOT *bows and exits.* ROGER *stands pale and still at the extreme right of the stage.*

HENRY. Dear Christ, the day that any man would dread
Is when life goes separate from the man,
When he speaks what he doesn't say, and does

What is not his doing, and an hour of the day
Which was unimportant as it went by
Comes back revealed as the satan of all hours,
Which will never let the man go. And then
He would see how the natural poisons in him
Creep from everything he sees and touches
As though saying, 'Here is the world you created
In your own image'. But this is not the world
He would have made. Sprung from the smallest fault,
A hair-fine crack in the dam, the unattended
Moment sweeps away the whole attempt,
The heart, thoughts, belief, longing
And intention of the man. It is infamous,
This life is infamous, if it uses us
Against our knowledge or will.

[*The light is leaving the stage.* HENRY *moves restlessly.*

I can hear the ice creaking on the river.
I could hear the horses on the frozen roads
In this taut air, half way from the coast.
How many days?

ROGER. Two, my lord.

HENRY. They should have been back.
Still have not come back. [*He faces the audience in anguish.*
Did not come.

[*He moves into the shadows. Enter a* MESSENGER. *He does not see* HENRY, *and stands for a moment undecided. Then he calls in the direction in which he came.*

MESSENGER. You said I should find the King here.

VOICE [*off stage*]. Is he not?

HENRY [*almost unseen*]. Speak from there.

MESSENGER [*moving*]. My lord—

HENRY From where you are.

MESSENGER. I've been sent to bring you the news from England.

HENRY. Be afraid. Be afraid to say why they sent you.
You will never heal your mouth all your life long.
Leave it to a man who's already incurable.
I'll deliver your message.—It's the arc of swords.
Becket is dead.

[*The* MESSENGER *is silent.* HENRY *gives a deep, low cry from the darkness. Suddenly he steps into the light like a madman.*

No men are fit to live, no-one in the world!
Foul and corrupt, foul and corrupt. All
Contagious. All due for death. Why should I spare
A man who can bear life and bring its messages?
They have made the King's name death.
It is treason now to breathe!

[*He has the* MESSENGER *in his grip as though he would kill him.* ROGER *goes to part them;* MARSHAL *enters.*

ROGER. This is useless, my lord, useless, let him go!

HENRY. Take him out of my hands, take the thought of him
Out of my mind. There's been no news, nothing was said.
It's only here in my head, it's only here
Behind my eyes—only in my thoughts?

MARSHAL. No, my lord.

[HENRY *turns and goes slowly away. At the farthest point he pauses, but does not turn.*

HENRY. Let no one living come near me.

CURTAIN

END OF ACT TWO

ACT THREE

ACT THREE

HENRY

GILBERT FOLIOT

ELEANOR

YOUNG HENRY

RICHARD

GEOFFREY

CONSTANCE, *Geoffrey's wife*

MARGARET, *Young Henry's wife*

ROGER, *Blae's son, now Chancellor*

WILLIAM MARSHAL

A CAPTAIN

PHILIP OF FRANCE

OLD WOMAN

FOUR REFUGEES

SOME COURTIERS AND SOLDIERS

ACT THREE · 1174–89

MARSHAL. For three years I watched him, living in his haunted mind. Three years, also, without a Queen: for the Queen was following her own fancies in Poitou, shaping her own dream of civilization. Alone, Henry tried to shake free of the shadow of Becket, going at last on a desperate pilgrimage of penance to Canterbury.

[*The crypt at Canterbury, lit only by a few candles.* HENRY *is on his knees. The sound of monks singing the 119th Psalm.* HENRY *rises and sits on a stone seat against a pillar. He is barefooted, in a pilgrim's robe.*

HENRY. It may be the day's first mass they are singing.
I can say the night has been crossed. Though you never know,
Crouching in prayers in this holy cellar,
Whether the light has broken
Or the night's as dark as ever.

Enter GILBERT FOLIOT

HENRY. Is it day?

FOLIOT. The first hour, my lord, yes.

HENRY. The monks still awake to aim their lashing.

FOLIOT. They're waiting for you, at the high altar.

HENRY. Come on, then.

FOLIOT. Should I let you make such a penance?
After three days of fasting, and twelve hours of vigil,
How can the body endure this discipline of rods,

Two hundred or more strokes from these seventy monks;
And some, my lord, who saw the Archbishop's death
Will give the rod their memory.

HENRY. Let it take away mine. I've stood enough
Of this perpetual shuddering of the nature
Which makes each day the moment before judgement.
Three years of it, the grinding of the thought,
Rat's teeth on the bones of the mind.
It was never my guilt, only in the rage of words.
But, if I think so, I diminish nothing.
I accept it all, if I can be rid of it all.
They're welcome to take their toll on my flesh
If I can be free of the world's loathing, and my
Self-sorrow. In Christ's name, let's go.

[*Exeunt* HENRY *and* FOLIOT.

[*Darkness. The chanting of the monks suddenly stops. A pause.*

[*Sunlight.* ELEANOR *with her Court at Poitou: the young queen* MARGARET; CONSTANCE (*Geoffrey's wife*). *Also* RICHARD, GEOFFREY, YOUNG HENRY *reading with his back to the others,* MEN *and* WOMEN *of the Court.*

ELEANOR. We are giving a new heart to the world
Here in Poitou, a new language for love,
Singers and poets with the tongue of Apollo,
Rivalling even France in the art of living.
We welcome Harry here, from the dark life
Of his father's kingdom. Here he will find the laws
Keep time in him like his own heart; for here
We govern as music governs itself within,
By the silent order whose speech is all visible things.
—But there is still business for this Court of Love.
How else can we define the world of woman
And man for you, before the Court adjourns?

COURTIER. Would the Love Court of Poitou consider
That true love can long survive in marriage?

GEOFFREY [*to* YOUNG HENRY].
You'd better give your attention to this, Harry!
Will our wives be judging themselves or us?

YOUNG HENRY. I had a cool enough welcome from mine.

GEOFFREY. You've been
Away too long. The girl has forgotten the touch.

YOUNG HENRY. The whole enrapt colony of them
Has forgotten what the world is like. They're asleep in the sun.

GEOFFREY. You seem to have overlooked the mind of our mother.
She has a finger on every pulse in Christendom.

YOUNG HENRY. There's only one pulse in Christendom, the one
Self-will, overriding everything: our father!

GEOFFREY. Ssh, quiet! They've come to a decision.
This is interesting.

ELEANOR. We are not unanimous.

GEOFFREY. There's my Constance!

ELEANOR. Nevertheless, consider
The nature of love. In love a man and woman
Are newly minted as in the beginning of the world,
Creating themselves out of each other's eyes.
But in marriage, whatever world is made,
Has the bones of the woman walled up in the foundations,
No air to breathe, nor any light to move in.

GEOFFREY. I reject the statement!
No abatement of love in marriage, an increasing!
And there's my wife, carrying for you
The bulky demonstration under her heart.

CONSTANCE. You are called to order! This is contempt of court.

ELEANOR. It's a happy wife who finds love and marriage consonant.

YOUNG HENRY. Will you listen to what I have to say? Will you listen?
In this drowsy hive you are all so in love with yourselves
No facts can penetrate. Do we mean to let
My father take all the world, and us with it?
At Canterbury I saw him whipped like a boy,
But, my God, now he has it all his own way.
However fast the rebellions come
Or the miracles flow from the dead Becket
They disappear like snow from the heat of his flesh.
At last I've got away from him: but if we mean
To have any independent life, we should listen
To what young Philip of France is saying. . . .

ELEANOR. There are murmurs of life still in this drowsy hive.
I have young Philip's confidence, and he
Has mine. Be with us here; you will come to know us better.—
Well, there we have the session's end.
Another day has gone ripening over the vineyards.
As the dew settles on the dust, contentment
Visit your evenings, and your sleep be untroubled.

[HENRY *is standing among them.*

HENRY. There is one more thing before you go.

YOUNG HENRY [*hysterically*]. If he tries to drag me back
To where I'm never given the powers that belong to me,
I swear I'll throw myself down from the walls
And finish what has never been a life anyway!

RICHARD. I've had no message that you meant to visit us.
Forgive us if we haven't a welcome ready.

HENRY. Forgive yourselves if I come like a man among enemies.

ELEANOR. It's my world that you step into here, Henry.

HENRY. I know this place of yours, Eleanor,
Where you nourish whatever can do me harm,
Where you corrupt the hearts of my sons against me,
And knit your fingers with any man who hates me.
I know your world, where an acid wit
Is valued higher than the mind hurt by it,
Where rules dictate how a man should move, or love,
Or cough, or betray, or do nothing:
The unexceptionable dance of what
Has withered within. Where every syllable's
Up for valuation by the code
Of the best poets, and nothing speaks from goodwill.
I have understood at last the truth of the text:
A man's enemies are the men of his own house.

ELEANOR. A man's own house is what he builds for himself.
Here you're in mine, which faces its own way
And looks towards other things.

HENRY. Not any more.
It has come to an end. You are under arrest.

[*The sons cry out in protest.* ELEANOR *sees* HENRY'*s soldiers beside her.*

ELEANOR. You take me back to yourself in the only way
You know, by forcible possession,
As you took your own vision of the world
With a burly rape in the ditch. Your hopes, therefore,
Are born bastards, outside the laws I recognize.
The true law hides like the marrow of the bone,
Feeding us in secret. And this hidden law may prove to be
Not your single world, not unity but diversity,
And then who will be the outlaw?

HENRY. A fine secret law
Which kills good faith among us! Yes, you can smile:

You think faith is a word I've no right to use.
But I can tell you, my love for women
Is more of a kind with God's laws
Than the aesthetic of adultery that you cultivate here:
And ever since Louis died
Political adultery with France
Is growing hot in all your dreams against me.
To which you add the violation of the minds
And hearts of these boys.
All this I'm bringing to an end.

ELEANOR. You imagine so.
You can accuse me of nothing, except of following
The free course of events, the new order of things
Which is growing up round us. You bring nothing to an end.
You have kept young Harry breathing no air but yours,
Sleeping, riding, eating, always in your presence.
Is he any the more yours for that? He made
His escape from you. And so did Becket.
For what part of Becket, after all, has been done away with?
Only his human failings. Now he is rid of them.
His argument has become an incorruptible statement.
Purpose, however wise, is hardly blessed.
God thrives on chance and change.

HENRY. God use his eyes on me, this is sophistry!
If Becket had wanted peace he could have had it.
What's my crime? A secure Plantagenet empire
And a government of justice. Am I to be
The only man who goes begging for justice?
And begging it from sons who will benefit the most.
Affection they never lacked from me,
Patience they've drawn on as if from a bottomless well.
Let them try and deny it: and blame themselves

If I have to use harder means to make them know me.
[*To the* SOLDIERS:] Take the Queen to our care.

ELEANOR. You can drag me with you wherever you pace the earth,
Or leave me shut behind walls, you will know I am there.
Not I the prisoner. You, within yourself,
Are the one roped, waiting for punishment.
The shadows will only deepen for you. They will
Never lift again.

[ELEANOR *withdraws, the* SOLDIERS *with her.*

GEOFFREY. Haven't you forgotten the prediction about our family?
What it is our blood inherits? Each of us against the other,
Brother against brother, the sons against the father.

YOUNG HENRY. That is one hereditary right you can't
Deprive us of.

RICHARD. You can't rob us of your nature.

[*Exeunt the* SONS. *The light changes. Enter* ROGER.

ROGER. Does a Chancellor, as fresh to office as I am,
Have a right to criticize his King?

HENRY. Any man has the right. But nobody
Can hit more painfully than my own thoughts.

ROGER. This is what I mean: this excess of grief
Against yourself is crippling your spirit.

HENRY. What did I do to lose them? First their love,
Then their lives? First Geoffrey, then Young Harry.
Geoffrey, a boy who spat with life
Suddenly by life spat away,
As though the fever said, like the voice of God:
'No more riding against your father.'
And then Harry, dying in a terrible anxiety
To have forgiveness. I doubt if a man
Can summon up enough grief to measure these things.

Enter RICHARD

RICHARD. Poor brother Harry. I have prayed that his soul
Shall be well received.
I imagine he is less perplexed now, taken
To the fountain-head. I shall miss the thought of him
Walking the world. I shall wonder about him.
We'll say no more. Death forgives most things.
I've come for your blessing, on my succession to England.

HENRY. You expect too much too soon.

RICHARD. I only expect
What's mine by matter of course. Unless you want
To make it a matter of war. Do I have to show you
By force that I'm first in the hierarchy?

HENRY. A wiser ambition would be to be first in my heart,
A place you refuse to fill. But you have still
One brother left. There is still John.

RICHARD. Oh, yes, there is still the favoured one!
I can see a day coming when I shall find
John has been conveyed into my place
And England already disposed of.

HENRY. I dispose as I choose.
By God, you'd better submit to my peace:
And shall, till a world comes which I have no part in.

[*Exeunt* HENRY *and* ROGER.

RICHARD. No, no, my father! Rather than that
I promise I'll drive you back across your life,
Town by town, over the road you have come,
Until I return you to your beginning
As lacking in power as when you were born.

[*Exit* RICHARD.

MARSHAL. Ordeal by generation. This, then, was to be the end of the universal argument: the ambition for the world transformed into private grief. Is he the man left following behind, crying out for justice, or the man living out his faults? I have no answer. I only know that Richard and young Philip together, drove us back town by town as he said he would. We fell back through the king's memories one by one. 'Here it was . . .' he would say; 'and in this place . . .'. But each time it was a grimace he looked at; he said so. The memory had been different. The streets were like furrows; or scars, rather; and we were driven out, leaving dead men slumped on the walls. Until at last we withdrew here, into Le Mans, the King's birthplace. A thick mist was over the valley of the river. We smashed the bridge, and as we started driving spiles into the fords the mist lifted. We saw the pavilions where Richard and the French army had spent the night spread along the edge of the wood only a few yards away from the river. When the King saw them, he turned to me as though to someone who should wake him from a nightmare.

A CAPTAIN [*entering downstage*]. Where is the King?

MARSHAL. Not far away. We shall soon have him with us. Stand ready. [*Exit* CAPTAIN.

. . . He told us to fire the houses beside the river, destroy cover and hold the enemy back. But the wind veered, and the flames leapt roaring through the ramparts, and took hold of the city. The citizens have poured out through the gates, and here we are now, seven hundred men, fallen back to the fields outside the walls.

[*Three* MEN *and a* WOMAN *come out of the burning city, pushing a handcart piled with their possessions.*

1ST. Will you come on? Your mother's dead, isn't she, and the fire's gone over her.

4TH. O God, God, blessed Mary!

1ST. Well, come on, then.

4TH. Where can we go?

1ST. All the rest of them's a mile on the road, aren't they? Tie the stubborn bitch to the cart.

4TH. Leave me alone.

1ST. Then will you move yourself? You'll see what comes to you when the French army's across the river and wants a woman. Walk, will you?

[*They move on. As they go, an* OLD WOMAN *enters, struggling along slowly, dragging a feather mattress and talking to it.*

OLD WOMAN. Ah, come on. What's the matter with you, you old feathers? You're not going to stay and be burnt. You'll come along with me. I haven't dragged you as far's this to lie down on you. It's to save you from the roasting.

MARSHAL. Here, you can't manage to take that along, old mother.

OLD WOMAN. I ought to manage. They was my own gooses. It took me seven Michaelmasses plucking them. And the feathers flew up light enough then, when they was wanted in the bloody bolster.

MARSHAL. Is this all that you've saved out of the city?

OLD WOMAN. I've brought away a spoon in my pocket; but the rest this old dreadful fire he can have it. Because he's sure to have it, after. As long as I keep the gooses' bed. In the end, I've had my days pretty comfortable. But there's my dying day I haven't had yet, and except for these gooses under me there won't be no other company then. So they can stop dragging and come of their selves.

MARSHAL. I'll take it a bit on the road. There's a cart ahead of you. [*He lifts the bed on to his shoulder.*] Ah Christ, your damn gooses! There's some burning smudge got into me!

[*He lets the bed slide to the ground, takes off his helmet and flicks away the smudge.*

OLD WOMAN. Won't you lift it up again? Ah, ah! How am I going to do, if the old devil has got into my bed?

[MARSHAL *kicks the bed flat, and stamps on it.*

Is the old devil dead?

MARSHAL. May God do the same for the cares that scorch the King.

[HENRY, *dazed and half-blinded, enters from the city.*

HENRY. There's no more to come from God! I've seen what God's mind is.

He knew I loved this city,
He knew if he ever looked into my heart,
He knew I loved the city I was born in.
And here my father lies in his grave. And I
Have thrust him in the fire.
I have burned my city, I have burned away
My own beginning, the one place in the world
Where memory could return untroubled, before
The earth began to bleed wherever I walked.

[*He looks up to the smoke-obscured sky.*

I meant the fire to save us! Do you think I kneel
To a God who can turn a brutal wind
To eat us up in fire? No,
I renounce all part in you: no such hands
As yours will have my soul. I'll burn it
Away like the city, I'll hurt you
In the centre of your love, as you do me.
Your eyes can sting like mine, and weep
With the same helpless water.
There's nothing left for either of us to save.—
We move out, Marshal.

MARSHAL. The men are waiting
Over in the meadow there, ready to stand or ride away.
All except Prince John. I thought he was with you.

HENRY. John not here? Damn him, it's a cool woman
Who can hold him down in this heat. But he'll be with us.
He's been close beside me all through these weeks;
He knows what has been endured, for the sake
Of his inheritance. How near have they come?

CAPTAIN. They're already wading the water, my lord.
Half Count Richard's men are across.

HENRY. This time
He's not going to find a forgiving father, but days
Of riding after us till we make a stand
With the fresh troops of Anjou.
All right, sound retreat. And tell your men
No carrying away loot. This ride will find
The weak seams in all of them, men and horses.

Enter ROGER

ROGER. The people who have left the city have turned back on the road.

MARSHAL. There's an old fording-place there if the French have found it.

ROGER. The way out is getting narrower.

HENRY [*to the* CAPTAIN]. We'll go through the woods. Halt at the first clearing.
I'll join you there.

[*A trumpet call.* HENRY *is suddenly as gay as though he were a boy again.*

That trumpet will bring John.
I know every crawling root and low bough of these woods,
Hunted and roamed it all over in my boyhood:
Path, and turn, and brook, I'll show you the ways.
And we'll shake off Richard, leave him confounded.

Come on; the years are only beginning.
We head for Anjou; with Angevin men we can start again.
I turn my back, yes, I turn my back,
But when I turn my face—Marshal, Marshal—
Where are the horses? Get me into the saddle.

[*He gasps with pain and grips the shoulders of* ROGER.

MARSHAL. Sir, we're ready; it's time to go.

HENRY. My own body now—my own body—

MARSHAL. What is it?

HENRY. —fights me. From the heels to the throat, Marshal!

MARSHAL. Lean on me. You'll crack the boy's bones.

ROGER. He can have my breath if it helps him.

MARSHAL. This is no place to stand. Walk these few paces. Come on, sir. The miles of the world have been nothing to you.

HENRY. Ah! Almighty God!

MARSHAL. Once through this you'll be back to everything you were.

HENRY. You think so, good.—But you don't know this pain! It hasn't—[*He pitches on to the gooses' bed.*] It hasn't a sense of mercy.

MARSHAL. You can defeat it, we must ride away.

HENRY. Cannot ride.

MARSHAL. Cannot? That has never been a word of yours, my lord.

HENRY. Cannot. It's mine now.

ROGER. Both armies are coming up: one out of the smoke, the other out of clouds of dust.

HENRY. Well, I'm here. And they come.

[*He turns in agony on to his face.*

ROGER. Look how his breathing tugs him, Marshal.

MARSHAL. He must lie there, though we love him.

[*A roll of drums from the left, answered from the right. The standard of Aquitaine is borne out from the city, the standard of France from the road. The clothes of the men are heavy with water.* RICHARD *comes forward, smiling, to* PHILIP *of France.*

RICHARD. We've come through that action, Philip France,
Like sheep through a dip, sweating and red as fire,
Damp as the water, but unscratched. Not a man
To receive us. What sheep-faced fools do we look?

[*He laughs, but* PHILIP *does not; his head turns, and his eyes rest on* HENRY.

PHILIP. Henry of England. Henry of England.

RICHARD. My father, God be with me! We have brought him down after all!

PHILIP. I was born to meet him at this moment. Wake him.

MARSHAL. He hears you, and knows whose voice it is.

RICHARD. It's the old dog's custom to take his sleep waking.

PHILIP. Does he mean to feed himself into the ground
Now that his greatness has been so humbled?
Tell him the time for that hasn't come yet.
There are things to be said between us.

MARSHAL. He's in too much pain.

RICHARD. He picks his time well.

MARSHAL. I'll come with you as a hostage; you can be sure
He will meet you tomorrow.

RICHARD. I love him for this!
He can use the quick swerve, the double back,
The dive for home, better than any ball player.
But only Lucifer knew how to fall and then

Come back into a kingdom. My father is only
Demon by descent. But he made the most of it.

HENRY. If a son can make his tongue goad at a father
My body can be made to stand. You shall have your conference.

[*He tries to struggle to his feet, but drops on to all fours, and moves towards them in this way.*

MARSHAL. Does this give you a pleasure you can bear?

PHILIP. Help him to his feet.

RICHARD. He's playing for pity
Trying to shame us into leniency.

[HENRY *gets to his knees, and then stands, putting* MARSHAL *aside.*

HENRY. Mind your own business, Marshal. Get it over,
You God-given boy. Get on with it.

PHILIP. You have come
To the end of the proud years, when all events were Henry.
An old man now, with your self-appointed sorrows
To keep you company; no longer fit
For the care of the many people. The time has come
To make good the years of insult you gave my father,
As well as other men of worth,
Not least your son here. God with his gradual purpose
Has brought us face to face.

HENRY. Spare us the piety.
What do you want?

PHILIP. First of all the homage you owe me,
Placing yourself in my hands without question.
You will give to Richard: Poitou, Maine, Touraine,
Anjou, and Normandy.
Release his mother, your Queen, and call on your barons
To acknowledge him as your successor.

You'll pay an indemnity of twenty thousand marks,
For all the destruction of this campaign. Meanwhile
The castles which have fallen to us in this war,
As well as the castles of the Vexin, stay in our hands
Until everything demanded has been done.

[HENRY *moves his head slowly towards* RICHARD.

RICHARD. This is all I ever asked. Except
For the indemnity, we make no other claims.

HENRY. All you asked. How much less is this than all?

PHILIP. The passing of years make their own justice.

[*Still* HENRY *broods. The air is heavy and silent. Then a long mutter of thunder.* HENRY *raises his head.*

HENRY. Whose is this offence?

[*A peal of thunder.* HENRY, *almost falling, is held by* MARSHAL.

Anything, anything. Stand back from me, Marshal.
And cover your ears. Further away. I am one
More who betrays the city.

[*He turns to* PHILIP, *his voice very low.*

You have my homage.
I can't get to my knees and up again, but you have it.
Everything you demand you know you can take.
That's done; the world has been altered; I can go.

PHILIP. We end the day with the kiss of peace, then.

[PHILIP *gives* HENRY *the kiss of peace.* RICHARD *comes forward to do the same. As he kisses his father,* HENRY *speaks softly.*

HENRY. You have a lesson to learn. Death can wait
Until your brother John and I have made you
A fair return for this.

RICHARD. My brother John?
And where do you suppose my brother John is?

HENRY. God forgive you. You've taken him prisoner.

RICHARD. Prisoner? John? My own dear brother? No.
He came over to us in the best of spirits this morning
To be on the side where the sun was rising.

HENRY. Liar!

RICHARD. Brother John is allied with his brother Richard.

HENRY. He knows we undertook all this for him.

RICHARD. Who's for a rest, Philip? My throat's as rusty
As the earth here.

PHILIP. There's a tent pitched in the field.
Water to wash in, and wine to swill down the dust.
Though in my spirits I could walk the world now.

[*Exeunt* PHILIP *and* RICHARD.

MARSHAL. Sir, sir, sir.

HENRY. That's all, that's all that was left
To come. The rest can go on, on and on
As it will.

MARSHAL. Give way, sir; lie down here.

HENRY. Give way, go down . . . they all say it: go down,
Give way, go down. [*He goes blindly on to the bed.*
Shame, shame, shame,
On a conquered king.

[MARSHAL *crouches beside* HENRY, *and makes a pillow of his cloak while he speaks.*

MARSHAL. You're only obeying
Your own body's knowledge of endurance
Which says Hold still for awhile, raging man.
Hour after hour, for thirty years,

You have shouldered up a world towards your mind,
Seen it thrown down more than once
As though for ever, and righted it, lifted it,
Borne it even higher. It would have broken
Twelve men's hearts, each of your own strength,
To have hewn their way through these years as you have.
The severe day begs for a little night to rest in.
Only a bruised, not a conquered King.

ROGER. Sir, believe what you've accomplished.
Your laws are fixed on England: grumbled at
Like the weather, but, like the weather, accepted
As a source of strength. The people have become
Their own law, in the twelve men representing them.
Unparalleled in Christendom, this new nature of the island.

HENRY [*in delirium*].
Hot on the road, eleven furlongs from Paris.
And now we're carrying half of France, the horse
Has good reason to stumble.

MARSHAL [*to* ROGER]. There's the fever talking.
I'll find somewhere where he can lodge before
The sun goes down. And out of the sound
Of that triumphant mob of France,
Singing there in the field, like a village wedding.

[*Exit* MARSHAL.

HENRY. The bells are ringing—do you hear them, father?—to celebrate my marriage. We've got the lustrous Queen. We can start creating the world. My sweat could lie with hers and breed rivers. It's too hot to ride any further. I'll get down into the water. There's my father, washing the filthy summer sweat off him.

[*He struggles to get out of his clothes.*

ROGER. Wait a bit, sir: your father's not there now.

HENRY. Yes, he is there. Father, stay where you are. I'm coming. The grime of the journey is fearful. We have to wash it off.

ROGER. It's all right, sir: there it is: you have had your bathe.

HENRY. No. By no means. I'm not washed clean. [*He shudders.*] The water's been lying in the dark too long. It's icy cold. The caked sweat and dirt goes in so deep you have to wash to the bone.

ROGER. You're well washed now. Feel the water on you.

[ROGER *guides the King's hand across the sweat on his body.* HENRY *turns his eyes to him.*

HENRY. On our way from Paris we bathed in a deep pool away from the sun. At night my father lay like this; in two days he was dead. Do you know who I am?

ROGER. The King, my lord.

HENRY. And who is this man the King?

ROGER. My father.

HENRY. That wasn't thought of when I got you. A bull night and an unfastidious whore, while the rain soaked through the tent. And by God's mercy you were made. I've done better things and been worse punished.

ROGER. I owe you a life, sir.

[ROGER *dries the sweat from* HENRY'*s body with a cloth. Enter two or three* MONKS. *They stand beside* HENRY.

ROGER. Why are you standing here? What do you want?

MONK. We have come a long way to reach the King. We come from Canterbury.

ROGER. Christ Church monks: this is no time or place for you.

MONK. We have found the King. And what better time for him to feel the troubles of other men than now, when he knows affliction? We have come for a grant of our rights. No one but the King can give us the justice we need.

HENRY. You must wait until I come to England. Don't think because you see me stretched here on the rack, you can extort unfair promises. I'll hear you when I return.

MONK. What sort of answer is this to men who have struggled five hundred miles to see you?

ROGER. You have heard the King. And you know he keeps his word. Go back to England, practise patience, he'll come to you.

[*The* MONKS *move away. One turns back, his face contorted with anger.*

MONK. By the merits of the blessed Thomas Becket, whose life and passion so pleased heaven, God will shortly do us justice on your body!

[HENRY'*s head swings away, and he gasps.* ROGER *rises in rage, but* HENRY *pulls him down to his knees. Exeunt* MONKS.

HENRY. We have to hear it. I know this will never lift off me. . . . When you can, write for me to the Prior, tell him I think with concern of the difficulties which are his. Say that meanwhile they should consider deeply of the two sides, and think well of peace. Say they did harshly, to bring Becket out of the grave.

ROGER. Yes, my lord.

HENRY. You shall have this ring: the Plantagenet leopard.

ROGER. No, my lord, no. The leopard has to stay on your hand.

HENRY. It has bitten deep into my finger. There it is.

ROGER. I'll not take it until you are back to power, both in body and kingdom.

HENRY. Only you of the brood haven't confirmed that all my affections were a fool's errand. . . . What are you saying?

ROGER. Sir, I was praying that God would soon return you to prosperity.

HENRY. The decision's already been made. There's no argument any more, and no more heavy blows between us. Go and call back that monk who cursed me with such pleasure that it made him tremble. Now he can absolve and bless me for his trouble. The formalities of allegiance. I believe in the law.

ROGER. Time for that when we've taken you to shelter.

HENRY. Call him now; while he still remembers me.

ROGER. I'll go when William Marshal comes back, my lord.

HENRY. Are you failing in obedience?

ROGER. I mean I can't leave you alone, my lord.

HENRY. What's the harm? I'm familiar with this place. Fetch him.

[ROGER *rises and looks into the growing shadows where the* REFUGEES *are crouching.*

ROGER. Good people, while I'm away watch over him.
You know he comes of your city, and you of his.
Take care of him as a neighbour, and if he calls for me,
Shout as you run to fetch me; I shall hear you.

[*Exit* ROGER. *The* REFUGEES *move a little forward.*

3RD. You know, this was the king of the world, so men say.
4TH. He is looking.

[*The* KING *and the* REFUGEES *gaze at one another.*

HENRY [*in great anxiety*]. I don't know . . .

1ST. What, then?

HENRY. . . . if the laws will hold.

[*The* REFUGEES *gaze.* HENRY *turns his head away from them. A violence attacks his body. He tries to pull himself up.*

It is all still to do!

[*He falls back, and is silent.*

1ST. Mary Virgin, but I think he's dead.

2ND. Shall I put my ear to his heart?

4TH. No, come away. You can't come close to a great king.

[*The* OLD WOMAN *is whimpering and praying.*

1ST. I wouldn't come close to a great king, but what we have here is a dead man. You've seen fifty like it or more. I'm thinking, we've had nothing from him yet, and he's lost us everything we had in this burning city. This dead fellow owes us a bit of justice.

2ND. But he's a dead man, so he doesn't pay.

1ST. Nor say No either. He doesn't refuse us. These things he has will only go to them who want nothing. Fôr anyway he'll be stripped before they bury him, and washed and that.

4TH. I won't stay and see you lay hands on him. [*Exit.*

[*The* 2ND *has nervously joined the* 1ST *in stripping the body.*

1ST. This is gold, do you see that?

OLD WOMAN. It's wicked work, it's wicked work.

1ST. We'll give you something, but shut your mouth.

OLD WOMAN. I won't have nothing of it. I'm only waiting here to have my gooses' bed.

3RD [*on watch*]. They're coming. Run, man!

[*As he runs past the cart he grabs some belongings.* 1ST *and* 2ND *take to their heels.*. *The* OLD WOMAN *sits with the body of the* KING, *gabbling her prayers.*

Enter WILLIAM MARSHAL, *carrying a hurdle; and* ROGER *with the* MONK.

MARSHAL. Mercy of God, look!

ROGER. O God in heaven! O my father! I should never have left him. I thought they were simple men, but they were devils. [*He turns on the* OLD WOMAN.] You sat watching this, without calling for help which would have brought me to him. Did they kill him before they robbed him? Which way are they gone?

OLD WOMAN. I told them it was wicked work they did, wicked work they did. But he died in his own time, before they came up close. He was dead when they came to him.

ROGER. They'll be brought back and made to suffer for it.

MARSHAL. It serves no turn. It was in his heart to give them a world. Help me to lift him.

[*They lift* HENRY *from the bed to the hurdle.* ROGER *takes off his velvet cloak and spreads it over the body.*

MARSHAL. 'Christ,' he said, 'we'll have no naked men.'

[MARSHAL *and* ROGER *carry* HENRY *away on the hurdle, the* MONK *following.*

[*The* OLD WOMAN *sits for a moment. She gets up and goes to the feather mattress, tugs at it, and begins to drag it towards the cart.*

THE END

REPRINTED LITHOGRAPHICALLY IN GREAT BRITAIN
AT THE UNIVERSITY PRESS, OXFORD
BY VIVIAN RIDLER
PRINTER TO THE UNIVERSITY